What readers are say~~ing about~~ in30minutes guides:

Google Drive & Docs in 30 minutes

"I bought your Google Docs guide myself (my new company uses it) and it was really handy. I loved it."

"I have been impressed by the writing style and how easy it was to get very familiar and start leveraging Google Docs. I can't wait for more titles. Nice job!"

Twitter in 30 minutes

"A perfect introduction to Twitter. Quick and easy read with lots of photos. I finally understand the # symbol!"

"Clarified any issues and concerns I had and listed some excellent precautions."

Excel Basics in 30 minutes

"Fast and easy. The material presented is very basic but it is also accessible with step-by-step screenshots and a friendly tone more like a friend or co-worker explaining how to use Excel than a technical manual."

"An excellent little guide. For those who already know their way around Excel, it'll be a good refresher course. Definitely plan on passing it around the office."

LinkedIn in 30 minutes

"This book does everything it claims. It gives you a great introduction to LinkedIn and gives you tips on how to make a good profile."

"I already had a LinkedIn account, which I use on a regular basis, but still found the book very helpful. The author gave examples and explained why it is important to detail and promote your account."

Dropbox in 30 minutes

"I was intimidated by the whole idea of storing my files in the cloud, but this book took me through the process and made it so easy."

"This was truly a 30-minute tutorial and I have mastered the basics without bugging my 20-year-old son! Yahoo!"

"Very engaging and witty."

Learn more about in 30 minutes® guides at in30minutes.com

Personal Finance For Beginners In 30 Minutes
Volume 1
How to cut expenses, reduce debt, and better align spending & priorities

By Ian Lamont

Quick Guides for a Complex World

Image credits

Cover design by Monica Thomas for TLC Graphics, www.TLCGraphics.com

Stock photographs: Introduction: Dreamstime. Chapter 3: Kenneth William Caleno

All other photographs, images, tables, and diagrams were created by the publisher.

Contents

Conclusion: 85

Introduction: Frank, Jordan & Stephanie

I'd like to introduce you to Frank, Jordan, and Stephanie. These aren't their real names, but their stories are all too real.

Frank, Jordan, and Stephanie are similar in many respects. They work at the same company, have the same job title, and have the same salary — $50,000 per year. None of them are married or have children. None of them have mortgages, crushing educational debt or outstanding loans.

You may think that their financial conditions are similar, too. $50,000 won't go that far in a city, but it's enough to live on. You may have a salary that's around the same level, or have friends or relatives who make a similar amount.

But here's the interesting thing about Frank, Jordan, and Stephanie: Even though they work the same hours and make the same amount of money, their personal finances are vastly different.

Frank's situation is the worst. Frank is always complaining that he doesn't have enough money to live on, and indeed, he was evicted from his last apartment. He takes public transportation to get to and from work, and spends less than $10 on lunch every day.

Jordan's financial situation is also precarious, but you wouldn't know it by looking at her. She dresses well, owns a nice car, and takes small vacations several times per year.

How can Jordan afford it? She can't. She keeps the creditors at bay by working a second job four nights a week, waitressing near her home. Needless to say, she can barely keep her eyes open during her day job.

Stephanie is the only one of the three who has a handle on her

finances. She has her own car, manages to pay off her educational loans on time, and has even started to build a nest egg, via her employer's 401(k) plan.

Small spending decisions have big outcomes

How can three people with identical incomes have such vastly different financial situations? Some of it relates to major purchases or household expenses, such as monthly car or rent payments. But people's financial health also depends on a myriad of small spending decisions, which, over time, can either accumulate into big shortfalls or massive savings. Understanding how this process works and making minor adjustments to maximize your lifestyle can save you thousands of dollars every year, and can help make your financial situation much stronger. It's one of the central teaching points of *Personal Finance For Beginners In 30 Minutes, Vol. 1.*

How to lose thousands on lunch

Consider Frank's mealtime spending habits. Going to the cafeteria or a nearby fast food restaurant costs less than $10 every day. It may not sound like much, but over the course of a year, those hamburgers, McWraps, and sodas add up. In just one year, Frank spends over $1,500 on his lunch excursions.

Many of his colleagues spend less than half that amount by brown-bagging it with healthier homemade sandwiches or leftovers and only the occasional fried treat. Cutting down on the fast food lunches won't eliminate Frank's financial problems, but it will make them a little easier to manage.

In Chapter 2, we'll go over how casual meals and other flexible expenses such as cable television, restaurant outings, and luxury purchases can be reduced. There are even some psychological tricks that you can use to make the cuts more bearable.

Free money for retirement?

At the other end of the spectrum, we have Stephanie's growing nest egg, which has been built through relatively small contributions to her company's 401(k) plan. Don't be put off by the awkward name of the 401(k) plan, which is derived from a section of the U.S. federal tax code. The plan is a simple method for saving for retirement.

Every week, Stephanie has 5% of her earnings (about $50) automatically deducted and placed in an investment account. Just like Frank's lunchtime expenses, $50 per week may not sound like much, and indeed, Stephanie doesn't even notice the difference. But over time the contributions start to add up — and in Stephanie's situation, they add up in a positive way. The weekly contributions are automatically invested in mutual funds that own baskets of stocks (such as Apple, Ford, and Disney), bonds, and other investments. Even though the money comes from her salary, the 401(k) contributions are not taxed before they are invested. They will also grow tax-free (withdrawals are taxed as ordinary income, however).

Further, like many employers, Stephanie's company offers a matching contribution of up to 5% of the employee's gross pay. In Stephanie's case, this means she is getting an additional $50 put into the mutual fund every week. That's about $2,500 in free money that's added to her investment account every year.

Stephanie's situation is covered in more detail in *Personal Finance For Beginners In 30 Minutes, Vol. 2.* I also show how Frank and Jordan are planning their retirement savings, including how much they've set aside and the types of mutual funds they have selected.

The core concepts of this guide

Frank, Jordan and Stephanie serve as real-life examples of how people on limited incomes manage their money. But there will also be explanations of basic personal finance concepts, advice on how to better manage your spending, and even tips on how to organize your records. By the time you get to the end of this book 30 minutes from now, you are going to have a different perspective on how to manage your spending and improve your long-term financial health.

The core concepts taught in this guide include:

- **Evaluating your priorities, spending, and assets** (Chapter 1, "Chapter 1 - Taking stock of your life & finances")

- **Identifying and pruning unnecessary expenses** (Chapter 2, "Reducing flexible expenses")

- **Trimming necessary expenses and obligations** (Chapter 3, "Reducing fixed expenses")

- **Organizing and tracking your financial life** (Chapter 4, "Chapter 4 - Managing your accounts & data")

Personal Finance For Beginners In 30 Minutes, Vol. 1 contains a lot of practical tips and common-sense approaches to spending. By the time you finish the last page, you will hopefully have a solid idea about how you can cut costs, better manage your debt, and establish smart spending habits that can potentially help you save thousands of dollars every year.

Disclaimer

Personal Finance For Beginners In 30 Minutes, Vol. 1 is not a substitute for professional financial advice. This guide will not rescue people who are deep in debt, or are facing major life events, such as heavy-duty medical expenses, bankruptcy, or the birth of quintuplets.

I will, however, describe some of the situations that can arise if debt does get out of control (see "What happens when you don't pay your bills" in

Chapter 3). There is also information on resources that you can turn to — and scams to watch out for.

If you do have a particularly complicated financial situation, or need advice on how to handle a financial crisis, you should contact an accountant, certified financial planner, or lawyer who specializes in tax or financial issues.

State and federal agencies can also provide help, or point you in the right direction. For instance, the usa.gov website offers specific tips for dealing with certified credit counseling agencies, and also includes links to a website that provides free credit reports from the major credit reporting agencies (see "How to get a free credit report" in Chapter 3). The Federal Trade Commission's website (ftc.gov) is another helpful source of information, and contains descriptions of things to watch out for, including outright scams.

I've rambled on long enough. Let's get started!

Chapter 1

Taking stock of your life & finances

The first step in planning for your financial future is seeing where you stand.

But don't whip out your latest bank statement and pay stub yet. Instead, I'm going to ask you a simple question:

What matters to you and your family?

Evaluating your life priorities

"Oh no," you say to yourself. *"I bought a personal finance guide, but instead of getting down to dollars and cents, the author is one of these touchy-feely types who wants to know about my inner child."*

Not so! By asking you what matters to you, we'll be able to better align financial decisions with your lifestyle. Practically speaking, this means you'll be able to spend money on what counts — and have a better idea about what to cut.

For instance, if your family lives for having fun on the water, then spending and savings should be focused around things such as swimming lessons, beach vacations, and saving for a boat. Things that aren't priorities can be scaled back or eliminated.

One way to focus on your priorities is to review a bunch of broad categories, pick the ones that matter most, and then list the specific activities or expenses within the key categories :

Category	Specifics	Category	Specifics
Arts		Media	
Business		Politics	
Career		Religion	
Community		Sports/recreation	
Education		Travel	
Family/home life		Other	

For instance, someone who prioritizes Business may list "home office", "seed capital", "truck", or "relocation" to support his or her dreams. If you are a fanatic about Sports, either as a spectator or participant, then "season tickets", "lessons", or "gym equipment" might be listed as specific expenses or activities you want to invest in. People focused on Education might list "Timmy's college fund", "tutoring for kids", or "grad school." Religion-focused activities or priorities might include "church fund", "mission", or "pilgrimage."

These are life priorities. Don't think that you will be able to fund everything right away. Taking part in a mission, relocating to another state, or leaving your job to go to grad school are serious decisions that might take many years to plan and save up for. But the important thing is identifying what those priorities are, and aligning your spending and saving to support them.

What if *all* of these categories have specific expenses or activities that are important to you? It's a common desire to "have it all." But when it comes to managing your finances and planning for the future, it's impossible to have everything ... unless you're Donald Trump (in which case you're probably not reading this guide!)

When listing specifics, don't include *fixed expenses*, such as paying back student loans or getting insurance for your car. While necessary, such expenditures aren't your personal life priorities. As we'll see in Chapter 3, fixed expenses *do* have to be addressed when it comes to making spending decisions. For now, you don't have to include them on your list.

Build your list until you are satisfied with the priorities it contains. Really make an effort to identify *true* priorities — things that you really want to be a part of your current life, or your future. Knowing your priorities will make it much easier to manage spending as well as planning for the future.

How much do you make?

Most people have income that's based on having a full-time job, or several part-time jobs. If you're married, you probably pool your income with that of your spouse.

A few may own small businesses, or rent out an apartment or vacation property. Some may receive special sources of income, such as a trust, royalties, disability benefits, pensions, or retirement fund distributions.

For the sake of basic financial planning, it's important to understand your annual *net income*. That's what you take home *after* taxes, social security, health insurance, and retirement fund contributions.

Gross income is your total salary + other sources of income, *before* taxes, social security, and health insurance deductibles are factored in.

The easy way to figure out net income is to look at a recent pay stub or the record of a workplace direct deposit to your bank account. Multiply your weekly, biweekly, or monthly take home pay so you have an idea of what your yearly take-home pay is. Adjust for taxes if you typically receive a refund or have to write a check to satisfy your tax obligations.

Let's do the math. If your pay stub shows that you net $1,000 every week after taxes, social security, health insurance premiums, retirement account deductions, etc., but you typically owe an additional $500 in state income tax when you file every year, your net income would be as follows:

```
($1,000 × 52 weeks) - $500
= $51,000
```

Adding up fixed expenses

Net income isn't the whole picture. If you project your net income at $50,000 this year, you'll still have to deal with additional required costs that may lop off thousands of dollars every month. These necessary costs are called *fixed expenses*.

For instance, you and your spouse may still pay for student loans, auto insurance premiums, and monthly mortgage payments. Other fixed expenses include:

- Rent
- Real estate tax
- Homeowner's insurance
- Medical insurance, bills, Rx costs, and copays
- Transportation-related costs (gas, car payments, mass transit, etc.)
- Telecommunication costs (phone/Internet/etc.)

- Groceries

Depending on your family or living situation, you may have some additional obligations:

- Kid-related expenses (babysitters, daycare, after-school programs, summer camp, etc.)
- Spending on home maintenance
- Pet-related costs

Looking at this list, you may let out an involuntary groan. How is it possible to truly focus on your life priorities, let alone plan for the future, with all of these obligations?

Here's the thing: While it's often impossible to completely *eliminate* fixed expenses, there are ways to *reduce* specific items. Transportation costs, telecommunications bills, and even mortgage payments can be changed to bring down the financial burden and set up situations for saving. I'll discuss specific tactics in Chapter 3, "Reducing fixed expenses."

But some fixed expenses are truly fixed. For instance, if you own a home, then real estate taxes, homeowner's insurance, and certain maintenance costs are part of your financial picture. Likewise, you can't blow off federal taxes, unless you are willing to renounce your citizenship and buy a one-way ticket on a Panamanian-flagged schooner headed for the South Seas. These types of expenses simply have to be factored into your household budget.

Growth of income and expenses

Income and fixed expenses seldom stay the same.

You may get a boost in salary from an expected promotion, bonus, or cost-of-living increase. Your work income will drop if you plan on retiring next year, but you may be able to tap into retirement funds and social security to make up the difference.

Fixed expenses may jump if you are expecting a baby, if your older kids are starting college in a few years, or the interest rate on your mortgage or home equity line of credit rises.

It's not necessary to work out your net income and anticipated expenses over the next 5 years. However, if you know that a major life event is on the horizon, you should absolutely be aware of it and start planning.

What are assets?

Your house, the cash you have in your checking account, the car in your driveway, the oak table in your dining room, the pair of running shoes in your closet, and the phone in your pocket are all considered "assets."

However, when it comes to personal finances, *assets* typically refer to big-ticket items — houses, cars, boats, rental properties, precious metals, bank accounts, retirement accounts, etc. Your running shoes, beer steins, old Madonna albums, and a football with Tom Brady's autograph may hold great personal value, but they may not be worth much on the open market. Indeed, they may be hard to value, much less convert to cash. Other assets may have cost tens or even hundreds of thousands of dollars (a college diploma) but cannot be converted back to cash.

For certain assets, you may have only a partial ownership. A house is a typical example. Unless you've bought it outright, or until you have paid off your mortgage, you only have a limited amount of *equity* in the property. For instance, "I have 30% equity in my condo" or "I have $100,000 worth of equity in my house" reveals the amount you have paid for. The remainder is still owned by the bank.

What if you don't have any assets beyond that beer stein collection or a copy of Madonna's *Vogue* in mint condition? That's OK … this book is written for people who want to build up their assets, and improve their long-term financial health.

Summary

We started this chapter taking a look at your life priorities — the activities and expenses that are important to you and your family. In a perfect world, you would have more than enough money to spend on these priorities. What's left over could be put into savings for the future.

Unfortunately, most people don't have that kind of flexibility. After fixed expenses such as groceries and rent are subtracted from net income, there may not be much cash to spend on the things that matter … much less save for the future.

But there is hope. In the next chapter, I'll show you some easy ways to cut costs and change your attitudes toward spending.

Chapter 2

Reducing flexible expenses

Now that you have a better idea of your priorities, income, fixed expenses, and assets, let's turn to the category of spending that trips up millions of people every day: *flexible expenses.*

What is a flexible expense? Unlike fixed expenses, which are necessary household expenses and obligations such as taxes, a *flexible expense* is something you don't need to buy. Let's look at an example.

Exhibit A: Frank's lunchtime excursions

Remember Frank? He's the guy from the introductory chapter who has serious financial problems:

> Frank is always complaining that he doesn't have enough money to live on … and he was evicted from his last apartment. He takes public transportation to get to and from work, and spends less than $10 on lunch every day.

Let's talk about that phrase — "spends less than $10 on lunch every day." Doesn't sound like much, does it? But let's do the math. A few simple calculations reveal a big problem:

```
Average lunchtime meal cost: $7.50 per day
Weekly cost: $7.50 × 5 weekdays = $37.50
Monthly cost: $37.50 × 4 weeks = $150
Annual cost: $150 × 11 months = $1,650
```

(This model assumes 20 weekdays of lunchtime spending in a typical month. It also assumes no lunchtime spending during holidays, vacations, and sick days, which total about 1 month per year for Frank.)

You probably know someone like Frank. You may *be* Frank! And even if you're not, you probably realize that $1,650 is a *lot* of money.

I am not Frank!

I can hear your protests: "Wait a minute. I am not Frank! I only spend money at the cafeteria or go out for lunch about two or three times per week. And I never splurge."

Let us return to our friend, Mr. Math, to understand what this means in terms of actual spending levels:

```
Average lunchtime meal cost: $5
Average weekly cost: $5 × 2.5 days = $12.50
Average monthly cost: $12.50 × 4 weeks = $50
Annual cost: $50 × 11 months = $550
```

You may not be Frank, but $550 isn't small change, either.

Cheaper alternatives

Of course, the lunchtime alternatives to going out to a fast food restaurant or cafeteria cost money, too. But the costs are far easier to deal with.

Stephanie, Frank's colleague, rarely goes out to lunch. She always brings something from home, and joins her friends in the cafeteria or eats outside in a nearby park.

A single leftover meal might cost a dollar to cover the raw materials that went into preparation. A bag lunch with a homemade ham and cheese sandwich, a piece of fruit and a small bag of pretzels (all bought at the supermarket) might cost $2. A few times per week, Stephanie buys frozen meals at the local supermarket for an average of $2.50 apiece. Let's do the math:

```
2 frozen meals × $2.50 = $5
2 bag lunches × $2 = $4
1 leftover meal = $1
Total weekly cost: $10
Monthly cost: $10 × 4 weeks = $40
Annual cost: $40 × 11 months = $440
```

Compared to Frank, Stephanie spends $1,210 less every year. She puts that extra money to good use, by creating a special savings account for emergencies as well as taking full advantage of the retirement plan offered by her employer.

Small costs, big impact

After learning about Frank and his lunchtime spending habits, do you see how supposedly small costs can lead to sizable expenditures over time? Over the course of a year, these lunchtime excursions can really take a bite out of a person's financial health. For the Franks of the world, a seemingly innocent daily routine can turn into a financial drag that impacts other parts of their lives.

When you consider that most people maintain these habits for 5 years, 10 years, or even longer, it can lead to lost opportunities to save money, plan for retirement, or make purchases that *really* matter (remember those life priorities you listed in Chapter 1?)

I'm not saying that you should brown-bag it every day. Going out every once in a while can help break up the monotony of leftovers, sandwiches and cheap frozen meals. A lunchtime trip to the local diner or sub shop is also an opportunity to chat with coworkers, or butter up your boss. But is it really necessary to go out every day, or even three days per week? For most people, the answer is no.

To address this particular problem, an easy approach would be to cut the frequency of excursions by half, while reducing the average cost. Going out every other day would be a starting point, along with drinking free water at the restaurant or cafeteria, instead of soda or juice.

But if you have particularly aggressive financial needs, you may need to take drastic measures. Frank, who has been evicted in the past, falls into this category. Going on biweekly lunch excursions — or even cutting out paid lunches altogether — are far more sensible approaches.

A psychological trick to cut costs

It's hard to break routines. Slamming the brakes on spending, or cutting out something you've grown used to, can really feel like going cold turkey.

One approach to soften the blow is to "reward" yourself with something else, so it *feels* like you're getting something in return for changing your habits.

Frank could reward himself with a nicer meal once per month (for instance, the $20 seafood pasta special at his favorite Italian restaurant) in return for cutting out the daily fast food excursions. Doing this and bringing his own lunch from home not only makes him feel better about saving money, it also reduces his annual lunchtime spending by approximately $1,000 every year.

Let's do the math:

```
Annual cost of "reward" meals: $20 × 11 months = $220
Annual cost of self-prepared lunches: $440
Total: $660
Annual savings: $1,650 - $660 = $990
```

Dealing with other types of flexible expenses

When I started to write this guide, I attempted to make a list of expenses that people have to deal with in their day-to-day lives. The list quickly turned into a monster. I realized that it's impossible to list everything, considering people are so diverse in their life situations and personal needs.

Instead, I am going to concentrate on a few common flexible expenses that can suck up thousands of dollars each year. To complete your list of expenses (so you have a better handle on what these expenses are), take the following steps:

1. Get out a few months' worth of credit card statements and your checkbook ledger.

2. Grab the list of life priorities you wrote down after reading Chapter 1.

3. Go through the credit card statements and checkbook ledger. Write "P" next to any item that can be considered a priority, "E" next to any necessary, fixed expense, and "S" for special, which might be a one-time expense or special situation.

Anything left over is an unnecessary, flexible expense — and therefore a target of your cost-cutting efforts. Mark these with an "X"!

Cable/satellite/pay-per-view TV

According to the Television Bureau of Advertising, nearly 60% of U.S. households subscribe to cable television. More than 30% use alternate delivery systems, including satellite TV.

If you get full-service cable or satellite television, ask yourself the following questions:

- Do you really need hundreds of channels of programming?

- Are you actually watching those four premium services that you added on to your subscription package?

- Are your kids better off watching 10 hours of Nickelodeon and the Disney Channel every week?

- Are CNN and CNBC providing information that you can't get from the Internet for free?

The answer to these questions is almost certainly no. According to Nielsen, which tracks TV viewing habits, the average U.S. household receives 189 cable channels but only watches 17 of them. Yet people don't hesitate to shell out $100 or more every month.

Take a look at the extra charges on the following telecommunications bill, which piles on more than $50 in premium channel charges in addition to the $135 base price for Internet/cable/phone service. The grand total is $226 per month:

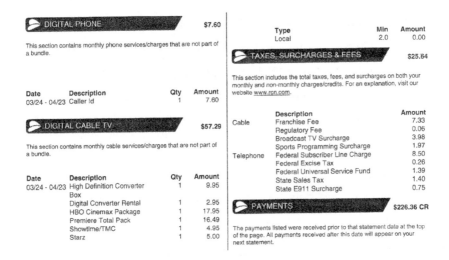

There are some situations which *do* require cable or satellite television. Residents of rural areas or distant suburbs may be too far away from broadcast towers to receive over-the-air broadcast signals. If you want foreign-language programming, you will need to pay extra. In some television markets, professional sports are *only* offered through a cable television subscription. And there are some people who can't imagine life without HBO or ESPN — they consider the dramas, games, and other programming to be life priorities!

But not everyone needs expensive subscriptions to premium channels. Millions of households would do fine with just the basic service package that brings in the nearest terrestrial broadcasters. A recent FCC study found the average cost of basic service is a little over $20 per month. For people who live near major urban centers, basic cable can be replaced by an antenna that plugs in to the back of a flat-screen TV. For a single one-time charge of $40, an antenna can bring in 20 or more digital television signals.

Exhibit B: Jordan's cable television bill

Let's compare Frank, Jordan, and Stephanie's bills. This comparison will let us understand the impact of television spending on their personal finances. For the sake of these comparisons, we'll leave Internet access out of the calculations (this will be covered later, when I discuss telecommunications costs in Chapter 3).

Jordan is a big spender, and likes everyone to know it. She has a brand-new 60-inch television, and gets an expanded basic service package from her local cable provider that costs $60 per month (not including Internet).

Jordan doesn't stop there. She has opted to pile on the extras. Here's how the costs break down every month:

```
Expanded basic service: $60
High definition converter box: $10
Digital converter rental: $3
HBO Cinemax package: $18
Premiere Total Pack: $16
Showtime/TMC: $5
Starz: $5
Franchise fee: $7
Broadcast TV surcharge: $4
Sports programming surcharge: $2
Total monthly cost: $130
Annual cost: $130 × 12 months = $1,560
```

It's a lot of money. Sadly, most of it is wasted. Jordan barely has time to watch TV. Thanks to her expensive tastes, she not only puts in 40 hours per week at her day job, she also has a waitressing gig five nights per week. Because she is seldom at home, the hundreds of channels she pays for are largely unwatched.

Exhibit C: Frank's satellite setup

Even Frank knows Jordan is paying too much. He has satellite TV, and subscribes to the sports package plus a few Spanish channels for his mom to watch when she visits every weekend. His monthly costs are more straightforward:

```
Basic service, including surcharges: $25
Spanish-language package: $15
Sports package: $8
Total monthly cost: $48
Annual cost: $48 × 12 months = $576
```

Exhibit D: Stephanie cuts the cord

Stephanie is far more frugal with her media spending. She has a pair of digital rabbit ears ($40) that plug into her HDTV. This pulls in 20 local digital television signals, including five public television channels, several national broadcasters, and the Country Music Channel.

She also bought a small streaming media box ($80). The box is about the size of a sandwich, and uses Wi-Fi to connect to her existing Internet connection in order to stream television programming to her TV set. Some of the channels are freebies, while others cost money. She gets the Internet-based service Hulu Plus to watch episodes of *Nashville*, *South Park*, and Jon Stewart's comedy show. She used to have Netflix (another Internet-based service) to watch other TV shows, documentaries, and movies, but felt that the selection was too limited. Instead, she now rents individual films through the streaming media box for about $4-$5 a pop. Here's how her annual costs break down:

```
Broadcast television: Free
Hulu Plus: $8 per month
PPV: $9 per month
Total monthly cost: $17
Annual cost: $17 × 12 months = $204
```

Stephanie's setup is actually well-suited to Jordan's needs. If Jordan decided to take her friend's lead, she would cut her annual costs by nearly $1,400, and still be able to catch occasional premium programming and movies via Hulu or pay-per-view.

Luxury spending: It's all relative!

You may think that "luxuries" refer to high-end branded goods that sell for top dollar — a $200 frying pan, an $800 leather jacket, a $2,000 computer, a $5,000 bicycle.

It's better to view luxuries as anything you can't really afford (and probably don't need). For some people, that may even include midrange brands or sale items that are too expensive considering income or cash on hand.

In other words, if you only have a few hundred dollars to spend every month after subtracting rent, living expenses, and other necessary expenses, even a $50 pan or $100 jacket can be considered luxuries.

"But it was on sale!"

I know someone who likes to shop. Let's call this person "Mrs. Lamont." When questioned about her luxury spending habits, Mrs. Lamont likes to fall back on the "but it was on sale!" defense.

Handing over a coupon at the checkout counter, or grabbing a high-end sweater for 50% off the original price may make Mrs. Lamont feel good. However, she's actually falling for tried-and-true tricks from the merchant to separate her from her hard-earned cash:

- The starting point for "discounts" may be the *MSRP* (manufacturer's suggested retail price) or an **arbitrarily high price that no one will**

ever pay. By crossing out the high price, retailers are handing shoppers a psychological victory that will make them feel good about the purchase, even if the discounted price is still expensive!

- Many shops have **loss leaders**, items discounted below cost that are intended to draw shoppers into the store. The retailer may be losing $20 on every purchase, but they hope to make it up with sales of other profitable items.

- Discounts tied to signing up for a store credit card allow retailers to **collect personal information** about customers and their shopping habits. This is great for targeted promotions and encouraging repeat visits. To top it off, if the credit card debt is not paid off in time, high-rate interest kicks in.

At the end of the day, taking 50% off a $250 dress still means walking out of the store $125 poorer. Resist the urge to use sales to justify unnecessary purchases of luxuries.

Living on credit to support luxury spending

When spending on luxuries gets out of hand, it impacts the amount of cash available to spend on other things, including necessities.

But the trouble doesn't stop there. For people who've used credit cards to support luxury spending, it's hard to pay monthly credit card bills in full, which leads to high interest rates (typically over 20%) on the unpaid amount.

Exhibit E: Jordan's credit card problem

A sobering experience for me occurred a few years ago, when I happened to see the docket at the local small-claims court. It was filled with a long list of banks that had filed suit against people who had stopped paying their credit card bills altogether.

Jordan may end up on the docket if she doesn't make some changes in her spending habits. She has luxury tastes, but can't fund them through her middle-class income. She's resorted to using three credit cards to fund luxury purchases such as fancy shoes and high-end appliances. She hasn't been able to pay off the amount owed for more than a year.

Now she's watching things snowball, as unpaid interest and further spending leads to ever-increasing credit card bills. Jordan owes $15,500 now, and it's still climbing. Eventually she won't be able to meet her minimum monthly payments, which will cause additional penalties to kick in. Failure to make payments will also make it hard to get credit from other sources, including bank loans. If things get particularly bad, she could find herself dealing with the situations described in "What Happens When You Don't Pay Your Bills" in Chapter 3.

Jordan's experience is not an uncommon one. According to estimates based on Federal Reserve data and other sources, nearly half (about 60 million) of American households carry a credit card balance that averages over $15,000 per household.

We'll return to Jordan's credit card situation in Chapter 3, when I give a big-picture view of debt and discuss practical ways to deal with it.

How to limit spending on luxuries

It may sound easy to limit luxury spending, especially if you are someone who doesn't do much shopping in the first place.

But if you have a shopping habit, or a family member who likes to buy luxury items, it's not so easy. Here are some tactics for taking control of luxury spending:

Set a monthly shopping budget: After determining your income and subtracting rent, food, healthcare, transport, insurance, and other necessities, and setting aside some of the remaining cash for savings and retirement, you should be able to budget the remainder to "other," including shopping. If shopping is a priority in your life, then allot more — but still stick to the budget. If you need help planning out your monthly shopping budget, consider some of the software tools described in Chapter 4.

Limit shopping trips: My daughter has a thing for shoes. If she steps into a shoe store, there is a 90% chance she is going to leave with a box of new shoes. The easiest way to limit her spending? Reduce the frequency of trips. The second easiest way? Paying with cash — preferably her own!

Use cash: When you use a credit card, you're using someone else's coin — usually the bank's, or the store's, if it's a store-issued card. Because the cash is abstracted through plastic and far-off monthly payments, it can seem like you're not paying anything at the moment of purchase. It's a mental trick that works against your financial interests. Fortunately, there's an easy way to counter it: *Start paying with cash*. The act of handing over a small stack of twenties to buy that fancy-shmancy kitchen gadget sends a pretty clear signal to your brain that your supply of money just got appreciably smaller.

Read the return policy before making a purchase: Think back to any item you've bought in the last few months that cost more than $100. Yes, I'm talking about that designer hat that looked good on the store mannequin, but on your head, not so much!

What was the return policy of the store you bought it from? You probably don't know, or would have to hunt for the receipt and look at the fine print. The next time you make a big purchase, look at the return policy (or ask someone) *before* you make the purchase ... and give preference to merchants who offer the best terms. If you have second thoughts or decide that the hat is not worth it, return it for a refund or store credit before the refund period expires.

How to limit online shopping

Retailers have clever ways of separating you from your money using the Web and mobile apps. They've removed barriers to spending by offering discounts, free shipping, and other conveniences. Amazon even has an app that lets you scan a barcode in a shop to see how much the same item costs on Amazon.com — then you can instantly order it!

The added convenience of online and mobile commerce can be hard to resist. Further, some of the tactics outlined above don't work in the digital realm. For instance, you can't pay online with cash. But there are a few tricks you can use:

Deactivate "one-click" or saved credit card settings: On most e-commerce websites, it's possible to save your credit card information. Amazon and a few other sites take things one step further, by enabling customers to make a purchase without reviewing the details of what's being bought or where it's being shipped. Deactivate the one-click settings and don't allow e-commerce websites to save your credit card details. Yes, it will require you to fish out your credit card when it comes time to complete an online purchase, but the added hassle will nip casual shopping in the bud while helping to prevent accidental or unauthorized purchases.

Force yourself to use a "cool-off" period: This is an easy way to force yourself to reconsider a particular purchase online or on your phone. Simply add the item to your virtual shopping cart, but don't complete the purchase for at least a few hours. When you come back to your cart, you'll have had some time to think about whether you *really* want to buy that brushed aluminum weed whacker or Hello Kitty handbag.

Restaurant spending revisited

How much do you spend at restaurants, food courts, pizza joints, company cafeterias, or airport sandwich kiosks in a given month?

We already saw how Frank's seemingly cheap lunchtime spending has drained his excess cash. For other people, weekly or biweekly restaurant dinners can lead to personal financial woe.

Let's do the math for a family of four who goes out (or orders in) five times per month:

```
Sit-down restaurant visits: $90 (average, inc. tip) × 2
= $180
Pizza night: $30
Chinese take-out night: $45
Weekend lunch buffet: $55
Monthly cost: $310
Annual cost: $310 × 12 = $3,720
```

I like eating out as much as the next person, but $3,720 is a *lot*. By cutting the frequency of restaurant visits in half, the family in this example could save nearly $2,000 per year (however there will be a small increase in grocery bills for the additional eat-at-home meals). Keeping an eye out for cheaper menu items or restaurant alternatives can also save money.

Summary

Flexible expenses include everything from too-frequent restaurant meals to cable television channels that no one watches. By cutting down on this unnecessary spending, it's possible to save thousands of dollars every year. It may require changing some ingrained habits, but as you've now learned, there are creative ways to reduce the pain.

Chapter 3

Reducing fixed expenses

In the previous chapter we covered various ways to cut down on the "extras" in our lives, such as the cable TV channels we seldom watch or the luxury goods that we can't afford. In this chapter, we're going to take a look at the fixed expenses that we have to deal with — car payments, mortgages, telecommunication costs, home energy costs, and more — and list some practical ways in which these expenses can be reduced.

Some of the tactics described in this chapter are relatively easy to implement, such as changing your mobile calling plan, or making some simple home heating and cooling adjustments. Others, such as refinancing a mortgage, require careful consideration and discussion with professionals such as your lawyer or tax accountant.

But one topic in particular requires a totally different way of thinking — cars.

Cutting car costs

Autos dominate our lives. We depend on cars for work and pleasure. We plan our cities and new homes around them. Even when we're relaxing in front of the television, advertisements for new cars are constantly paraded in front of our eyes.

Thanks to relentless media exposure and little-understood financing and sales practices, not to mention the perception of autos as important status indicators, most people replace their cars on a regular basis. A rent survey found that a typical new car-owner will keep a vehicle for nearly 6 years.

For many, there is no question that when they get their first vehicle — or buy a replacement car — it is going to be a *new* car. This is an accepted piece of wisdom.

If you follow the six-year buying pattern listed above, you probably will have purchased three new cars by the time you turn 40. Or, you may have fallen for the dealer pitch that urges customers to "lease a brand-new car for just $199 per month!" Of course, you have to read the small print to see that leases come with all kinds of gotchas, ranging from big down payments to restrictions on annual mileage. And you don't actually *own* the vehicle in a leasing situation. That means there's no trade-in when the lease is up.

While cars are a necessary, fixed expense, a fetish for new cars can lead to real financial pain. Fortunately, there are alternatives:

If you buy a new car, keep it longer. Recently manufactured cars tend to be vastly superior to the cars of decades past, in terms of resistance to wear, corrosion, and major mechanical failures. The old rule of thumb about the need to replace the engine or the car after it's been driven 100,000 miles has been thrown out the window in the latest generation of vehicles (as recently noted by the *New York Times* in an article titled *"As Cars Are Kept Longer, 200,000 Is New 100,000"*). This is party due to better materials and on-board technologies, but it's also because of an intense desire on the part of manufacturers to stay globally competitive.

What this means for you, the consumer, is a new car can be driven for 10 years or more if it's properly maintained. Heck, drive that sucker into the ground before you replace it!

Consider used cars. It's not necessary to buy a new car. You're often paying a premium for a new vehicle from dealers who will do *anything* to close the sale with a slew of extra charges, features, and fees that you don't need. Good used cars can be had for less than $10,000, if you do your research and shop carefully.

Recently built used cars vs. clunkers

If you've driven new cars all of your life, the term "used vehicle" may conjure up images of a dusty old beater with missing hubcaps and no A/C, dragging a clattering muffler down the boulevard. Yes, such cars exist, but I am not advocating that you buy one. Besides the embarrassment, there are also safety concerns and additional maintenance costs associated with clunkers.

Many used cars are actually rather new. The sweet spot for used cars *are models that are 1–4 years old*. That includes vehicles that are coming off of three-year leases.

Average prices for used cars, by category

The main advantage of buying a used car is saving money. Here's how Edmunds.com breaks down average used car prices for different types of cars sold by franchise dealers:

Type	Average	Type	Average	Type	Average
Compact Car	$10,572	Large Car	$11,330	Midsize Traditional SUV	$13,805
Compact Crossover SUV	$14,148	Large Traditional SUV	$19,051	Minivan	$12,851
Compact Truck	$13,387	Midrange Luxury Car	$21,574	Premium Sport Car	$42,943
Entry Luxury Car	$18,177	Midrange Luxury SUV	$29,763	Subcompact Car	$10,978
Entry Luxury SUV	$24,516	Midrange Sport Car	$28,251	Van	$13,714
Entry Sport Car	$17,321	Midsize Car	$11,729		

Keep in mind that these are *average* prices sold by *franchise dealers*. These cars tend to be newer and come with a higher markup than those vehicles sold by individuals, or those sold at auction.

Tips for buying used cars

When it comes to buying a used car, everyone wants a cheap, clean, reliable vehicle that can be driven another 100,000 miles. But for every 5-year-old Toyota sold at a discount by the little old lady down the street, there are 10 clunkers waiting for some sucker to bite. Don't be that person!

Here are a few tips for purchasing a used car:

1. **Get in the car, and drive it around**! Don't only take it around the block. Give it a real workout on city streets and highways. Try it out in various parking situations.

2. **Know the value of the car *before* you start negotiations**. It's easy to get prices online. Kelly Blue Book has an online database at *kbb.com*, or you can peruse your local Craigslist or classifieds for similar vehicles.

3. **Get the maintenance records or vehicle history**. The U.S. Department of Justice's National Motor Vehicle Title Information System (available at *NMVTIS.gov*) and the National Insurance Crime Bureau (*NICB.org*) have databases that can be searched by the car's Vehicle Identification Number (VIN).

4. **If the records aren't available, assume something may be wrong**. An eye-opening personal experience for me was talking with a franchise dealer about one of the cars on his lot, listening to him prattle on about how clean the car was and how it came from a local trade-in, and then seeing the vehicle history — the car had actually originated halfway across the country.

5. **Watch out for lemons**! The U.S. Department of Transportation has a Vehicle Safety Hotline (1–888–327–4236) and the *DOT website* has information on vehicle recalls. Another good source of information: back issues of *Consumer Reports*, which can be found at many local libraries.

6. **Hire a mechanic to inspect the car**. This might cost a few hundred

dollars, but it can uncover problems that the seller either doesn't know about or is attempting to hide. Either way, it can steer you away from a lemon, or give you more negotiating leverage.

Tips for buying used cars from dealers

Used car dealers have a bit of an image problem. I'm not going to get into the stereotypes or horror stories, but let's just say there are additional considerations when buying a used car from a dealer:

1. **Check out the dealer's reputation.** Google is your friend. You can see if complaints have been filed with *local consumer protection agencies*. And talk with friends or family members who have purchased cars from local dealers *in the last year or two*.

2. **Assume each car on the dealer's lot is being marked up at least a few thousand dollars**. Yes, you can haggle the price down, but no dealer is going to sell a vehicle at a loss.

3. **Cosmetic improvements may hide serious defects**. You can bet the dealer has waxed the car and power-washed the interior. But that doesn't mean the car is in "excellent" condition. There may be serious mechanical or electrical problems that the dealer hasn't addressed.

4. **Dealers don't have to offer money-back guarantees for used cars**. If a dealer offers one, that's great — *but get it in writing*!

5. **The FTC requires dealers to post a "Buyers Guide" in every used car they sell**, including demonstration models. The guide has to include warrantee information (if applicable), as well as various consumer warnings. The Buyers Guide becomes part of the sales

contract, and overrides any provisions in the signed contract.

6. **Some states don't allow "as is" sales from dealers**. The list includes Connecticut, Hawaii, Kansas, Maine, Maryland, Massachusetts, Minnesota, Mississippi, New Jersey, New Mexico, New York, Rhode Island, Vermont, West Virginia, and the District of Columbia. Some other states have requirements that carefully define an "as-is" sale of a used vehicle.

There are many more things to watch out for when it comes to purchasing a used car from a dealer. To learn more, visit the Federal Trade Commission website at *ftc.gov*.

And remember: At the end of the day, a shiny lemon is still a lemon.

Controlling phone and Internet costs

If you've had the same mobile phone and ISP contracts for more than two years, you're probably paying too much for mobile phone service, and home Internet access as well.

Why do people pay too much for telecom services? It starts the day they sign up. The options are hard to understand, the salespeople and order forms push more expensive plans, and perhaps most importantly, phone and Internet access are services most people *must* have. These are necessary expenses!

Once the telcos and ISPs have you, they'll have you for a long time. We're creatures of habit when it comes to mobile contracts and the wires piping high-speed data into our homes. It's a pain to deal with transfers, installations, and customer service interactions, so we shrug and keep paying a premium.

How to save hundreds every year on phone bills

Here's the outline of an actual mobile phone bill. This person ... or should I say, *victim*, pays nearly $100 per month. Let's do the math for the plan, which includes unlimited talk and text minutes, and 2 GB of mobile data (used to download email, surf the Web, and use apps which are connected to the network):

```
Monthly voice/text cost: $40
Monthly data plan: $50
Total monthly cost: $90
Annual cost: $90 × 12 months = $1,080
```

The sad thing is, she doesn't need this level of service. She sends a few dozen texts per month, and has her phone set to use Wi-Fi at home, meaning her mobile data requirements are minimal.

To top it off, the plan she has was introduced many years ago, when people were willing to pay a lot more for their smartphone plans. She could easily downgrade to a $40 per month plan offered by a rival carrier that offers unlimited calls and texts and more than enough high-speed mobile bandwidth for her needs (500 MB per month). Let's do the math on the costs for the $40 per month plan:

```
Monthly cost: $40
Annual cost: $40 × 12 months = $480
Annual savings: $1,080 - $480 = $600
```

What's a family plan?

Another option is a *family plan*. These plans let people group two or more mobile phone lines to a single bill, at a steep discount compared to what the plans would cost if they were paid individually.

The carriers will happily help you migrate phone numbers from other companies to the new family plan, and either set up new phones or switch out the SIM cards in the old phones (this may not be possible for all models, however).

Here's how a real plan works. It offers unlimited voice and texting, plus 1 GB of mobile data at the highest available speed for three separate mobile telephone numbers:

```
Two-line family plan: $80
Additional line: $10
Additional taxes & fees: $17
Total cost: $107 per month
```

Note that this does not include the cost of the phones. Nevertheless, the monthly cost for three lines matches the price that some people pay for a single line!

To cut down the cost of a family plan, go for the lower data caps (usually not a problem if you have Wi-Fi at home or at work) or use cheaper phones.

Contract vs. pay-as-you-go plans

Two-year mobile contracts are a ripoff. You're locking yourself into a plan that is probably not competitively priced, and will likely cost thousands of dollars over the life of the contract.

That's right, thousands of dollars. Let's do the math:

```
Monthly voice/text/data charge: $80
Two-year cost: $80 × 24 = $1920
Discounted midrange phone, offered with 2-year contract:
$100
Total: $2,020
```

Of course, cheaper plans are available, but the minutes and data allotments are extremely limited. Many people actually pay more expensive rates. I have friends and relatives who pay more than $100 per month for a single mobile line, because they don't know where to find cheaper plans or choose the options that fit their needs.

Prepaid plans

Pay-as-you-go, "prepaid" and "no contract" plans usually involve paying up front for a large block of minutes. For instance, one popular plan charges $25 for 250 minutes, which expire after 3 months (the expiration date can be extended if you purchase another block of time). You can top off the minutes using a credit card or a prepaid card sold in a store. If you decide to drop out of the plan, all you have to do is stop paying for minutes.

While the per-minute rates are expensive, for people who don't talk or text much, the plans are actually much cheaper than a phone on a two-year contract. However, you're pretty much limited to using old-fashioned feature phones that can only handle phone calls and texting.

Let's do the math:

```
100 minutes of prepaid time (3 month expiration): $25
Initial purchase + 7 refills over 2 years: $200
Feature phone cost: $30
Total two-year cost: $230
Savings vs. two-year contract: $2,020 - $230 = $1,790
```

I used prepaid phones for ten years, and saved many thousands of dollars compared to friends, relatives, and colleagues who had expensive two-year contracts. However, I eventually switched to an inexpensive monthly plan. The reason: I needed the features of a smartphone, which requires data to use the apps and email.

Monthly plans

Plans that don't require a contract and let users pay month-to-month have gained in popularity. The prices can be very competitive compared to two-year contract plans. However, you won't get a subsidized phone included in the price — you'll either have to bring your own, or pay full price.

Let's do the math for a pay-by-the-month plan with unlimited talk and text, and 500 MB of high-speed data:

```
Monthly charge: $50
Two-year cost: $50 × 24 months = $1,200
Midrange smartphone, full price: $250
Total: $1,450
Savings vs. two-year contract: $2,020 - $1,450 = $570
```

Saving money on new phones

Mobile phones can be expensive. Some carriers factor the price of the phone into the monthly bill, but others let customers pay for the phone up front and pay for wireless coverage as a separate bill. The newest luxury models with the biggest screens and best cameras can cost well over $500, but there are plenty of decent midrange phones that cost $250 or less. Cheapo models that only do calls and texting (also known as "feature phones") can be had for $50 with some calling plans.

What phone should you buy? Many people make their choices when they walk into the store or kiosk and look at the display models. This is a poor way to choose. While you, the customer, can evaluate the look and feel of the phone hardware that way, there's not enough time to adequately test critical features such as:

- Reception

- Responsiveness of the phone when fully loaded with apps and data

- Camera quality

- Battery life

- Operating system integration (particularly for Android models)

- How well certain apps work with the handset

In terms of evaluating reception, most carriers have coverage maps on their websites, but those can be unreliable. A better way to find out whether the phone can send and receive calls from where you live or work is to ask neighbors, colleagues, and others. I've seen people use Facebook, Twitter, and email to survey other people about specific devices and carriers.

As for the other criteria, there are a few ways to research phones before deciding which one to buy:

- **Determine how your personal needs may impact your selection of a particular model**. Are you a heavy-duty texter or emailer? Then a phone with a larger screen or physical keyboard may be the best choice. Similarly, if you like to take photos, then buy a phone with a decent camera and lots of storage.

- **Ask people with similar needs about their phones, and try them out!** People can usually describe what's good and bad about their phones. However, if a friend bought the phone more than a year ago, note that it may no longer be available ... or it may be missing features that the latest generation of phones includes.

- **Check the review sites and gadget blogs.** You have to be careful here, because some "review" sites do little more than rewrite press releases from the major phone manufacturers and carriers. Look for sites and blogs that contain long reviews and original photos.

- **Read the user comments.** Checking out what other customers have said online (for instance, on Amazon.com) can be tricky. How can you be sure "Roger53" is real, or knows what he is talking about? The answer is: you can't. But if Amazon lists Roger53 as a "verified purchase", and he and ten other users are all complaining about how the battery starts to lose its charge after a few months, that's a red flag.

- **Is the extra cost worth it?** Some manufacturers use the power of their brands to charge a premium that costs hundreds of dollars more than competing models. If two phones match up in terms of features, but one is $200 more expensive than the other, why would you buy the pricier model?

After doing any online research, make sure that the phone is available in a local retail or carrier shop. Why? It will give you a chance to do an in-person test of the basic features and feel the phone in your hand before you put down your hard-earned cash.

Finally, note that certain types of phones are associated with certain types of plans. For new or high-end models, you may have to agree to be locked in to a two-year contract, or pay high monthly carrier charges (plans for Apple iPhones are particularly expensive). Be sure you understand these restrictions before making your purchase.

Saving money on Internet service

Home Internet service is a necessity for most people. Internet service providers and cable companies know this. To get you to pay more, they offer "bundles" that combine Internet, phone, and cable TV. If you only want one of these services, the price is steep — at least $50 or $60 (and sometimes more, if there is no local competition).

Let's do the math on an Internet plan that does not include phone or television:

```
Monthly rate: $60
Cable modem rental: $8
Total monthly cost: $68
Annual cost: $68 x 12 months = $816
```

The bundles may seem like a deal — just $99 per month for all three! That's not much more than paying for one service at a time, right?

Not so fast. There's a catch with these bundles. Actually, there are several catches:

- *"Equipment, installation, taxes and fees are extra."* These fees are unavoidable, and bump up the price well over $100 per month.

- The basic bundle seldom includes everything you want, particularly when it comes to cable television channels. Even local broadcast television channels may not be included!

- Internet speeds may be limited.

- Phone service may be limited to local lines; out-of-state area codes cost extra.

- The rate does not include the cost of renting a cable modem

- Rates increase regularly — sometimes as much as $15 per year

All of a sudden, the $99 bundle costs $140 per month to get to the service levels you want for Internet, phone, and cable TV. Let's do the math:

```
Annual cost, first year: $140 x 12 months = $1,680
```

That's not all. The price of the monthly bundle usually jumps after 12 months, and sometimes jumps again after 24 months. I saw one $89 per month bundle that includes Internet, cable TV, and a few premium channels rise to more than $200 after 2 years. Here's how the bill breaks down when the customer starts paying full price:

```
Monthly cost for cable TV: $90
Monthly cost for high-speed Internet: $70
Monthly cost for premium channel package: $25
Additional monthly taxes, fees, modem rental, and other
charges: $20
Total monthly cost: $205
Annual cost: $205 × 12 months = $2,460
```

But there are ways to save serious money.

- *Get your own cable modem if you are handy with computers*. They cost $20 to $30, and you will have to install and configure it yourself. Savings: $60 in the first year, nearly $100 per year thereafter.

- *Don't get extra cable channels beyond the basic service*. You will be able to get premium programming through your Internet connection using Netflix, Hulu, Amazon Prime, and other services.

- *Negotiate with the ISP or cable company*. In the past, I've asked for and received discounts from telecom providers. The best time to do this is when you have a better offer in hand *and* the original contract (typically 2 years) is over.

How to haggle for Internet service

The point about about having a better offer in hand is worth explaining. Sometimes it may be a direct mail coupon that a local cable company or ISP sends you, or an ad that you see in the local newspaper or online. With an offer like this, you can go to your existing company and ask them to match it, or threaten to leave. I've tried it, and it really can work.

However, if it doesn't, you can always take up the other company on its discounted offer. This happened to me a few years back. Verizon increased the rate for my Internet/phone service from $80 per month to $100, and refused to cut back — they insisted that none of their new packages supported $80 per month. Fortunately, one of the local competitors was in the midst of a fiber rollout in our neighborhood, and was mailing out some incredible offers, including a $20 per month Internet offer. I checked it out. The rate rose to $35 per month in the second year, and $55 in year 3, but the contract only lasts for two years. The cable modem cost $8 per month, but I decided to get my own for $20.

Let's do the math:

```
Year 1: $20 × 12 months = $240
Year 2: $35 × 12 months = $420
Total cost for years 1 and 2: $660
Annual cost thereafter: $660
```

You'll notice that I did not get phone service. While I like having an old-fashioned phone for the better quality and safety (it's easier to dial 911 on a wired phone), the mobile phones we have seem adequate, so we decided to get rid of the landline.

Here's a final piece of advice: If you get a mailer that has an Internet offer that seems too good to be true, read the fine print to make sure that the deal you are getting into isn't worse than the one you have now. Remember that a $99-per-month bundle can turn into a $200-per-month monster in a few years. The impact on your bank account can run into many thousands of dollars.

Controlling other utility costs: the 10% solution

When it comes to saving on other types of utility bills, the experts tend to get into home improvement projects such as adding insulation to your attic, installing double-glazed windows or energy-efficient heating systems, or caulking every last crack and crevice.

That's great if you are handy with tools or happen to be on a first-name basis with the staff of your local hardware store. But for the rest of us, **I advise a much simpler approach that I call the 10% Solution.** Here's how it works:

1. Determine the sources of spending on electricity, gas, heating, air conditioning, and hot water.

2. Reduce consumption by 10%.

That's it. Find those things in your house that consume energy, and then cut consumption by just 10%. For example:

- If you usually take a 10-minute shower, cut it down to 9 minutes.

- Reset your thermostat to be a little warmer in summer, and a little cooler in winter.

- If you have a programmable thermostat, set the air conditioning and heating systems to power down a little earlier than usual. For instance, in the winter, we set our home's internal temperature to drop after 10 pm when we are in bed and under the covers. We program the thermostat to increase the temperature by 4 degrees the next morning before we get out of bed.

- Check your hot water heater's default temperature and drop it by a few degrees.

- When it's time to replace lightbulbs, get slightly lower-wattage bulbs or energy-efficient alternatives.

- Conserve energy in the kitchen, especially when using the stovetop or heating hot water (microwaving hot water or using a British-style electric kettle are not only faster, they are much more efficient than using a gas or electric range to boil water).

Taking slightly shorter showers, turning down the A/C by a few degrees, or making other tweaks to the ways in which you use energy are hardly noticeable. But they can save hundreds of dollars per year in power, gas, oil, and other energy costs.

Reducing debt-related expenses

When it comes to mortgages, credit cards, and other forms of debt, some people throw up their hands and assume the monthly payments are an unavoidable part of life.

In one sense, this feeling is understandable. Monthly mortgage payments and credit cards are obligations that cannot be shirked. However, there *are* scenarios that allow some people to legitimately reduce their payments. They include refinancing and transferring credit card debt to other cards with lower interest rates.

Refinancing your mortgage

Refinancing may be a way to reduce your monthly mortgage payments. But there are important considerations when refinancing, and you should always consult with professionals (such as your tax accountant and a real estate lawyer) before signing the "refi" paperwork.

Mortgages explained

If you've purchased a house or condo, you probably had to take out a mortgage. Mortgages are loans from banks that help homebuyers pay the difference between the cash they have available to pay for a home and the actual cost of the home.

Typically, mortgages have to be paid back in monthly installments over 15, 20, or 30 years. The monthly payments are usually equal (exceptions include adjustable rate mortgages, described below), and include principal as well as interest that the bank charges.

The size of the monthly payment depends on the amount of the principal, the length of the mortgage, and the interest rate offered by the bank at the time the mortgage started. Here's how a $200,000, 30-year mortgage at a fixed 6% interest rate breaks down:

Monthly principal and interest payments: $1,199
Annual principal and interest: $14,389
Total interest over 30 years: $231,676
Total payments over 30 years: $231,676 + $200,000 =
$431,676

The principal declines gradually over 30 years, until the mortgage is paid off:

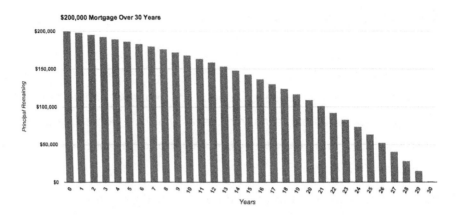

This is a greatly simplified view of mortgage payments. Not shown in the data above:

- Even though the monthly payment never changes, interest payments are high during the early years of a mortgage. Toward the end of the 30 years, most of the payments will be paying back principal.

- Local real estate taxes are not included.

- There are fees related to setup, late payments, and other situations.

- Lenders are required to reveal the annual percentage rate (APR), which is the mortgage rate plus fees, points, and some closing costs. If there is a big difference between the quoted rate and the APR, watch out!

Another risky situation that can lead to serious pain down the road involves monthly payments which "balloon" after a set number of years, which is typical of adjustable rate mortgages (ARMs). Here's a typical offer:

Many homeowners who are in the process of refinancing or purchasing a home have taken advantage of the new **Government Insured Low Rate Mortgages** available today. What does that mean to you? **You too can lock in to these government insured rates while they remain at historic lows!** As a HUD approved direct lender, Maverick Funding Corp Nmls #7706 has pre-qualified you for a loan of up to $240,000.00. Your new mortgage payment may be as low as $995.74* with a FHA 5 year ARM rate of **2.88% (3.07%APR)*!**

Let us show you how your pre-qualified status makes it easier to get the money you need to consolidate high-rate bills and keep more of your hard-earned cash – even if you never qualified before … and even if you have less than perfect credit! **But you must act now!** Your pre-qualified status - and the FHA's expanded loan limits wan't last long So please call us at 1 888 250 4282 today If you thought you waran't eligible

The initial rate is low, but the rate after the first 5 years is unknown. There is a real risk that the rate could more than double in the 6th year, which would greatly increase monthly payments.

You should always understand the terms of a mortgage based on the printed documents you sign as well as professional advice from an accountant, housing counselor, or experienced real estate lawyer.

Why refinance?

The main reason to refinance is to take advantage of lower interest rates. Refinancing can not only reduce the amount of interest you pay over the life of the loan, it can also lower your monthly bills, sometimes by significant amounts. Let's do the math on the example given earlier, but this time at a 4.5% interest rate:

```
Monthly principal and interest payments: $1,013
Annual principal and interest: $12,160
Total interest over 30 years: $164,813
Total payments over 30 years: $164,813 + $200,000 =
$364,813
Savings vs. 6% mortgage: $431,676 - $364,813 = $66,863
```

Here is the principal/interest breakdown for the two mortgages. Note how the payments for the 4.5% mortgage, taken in aggregate over the life of the loan, are mostly principal. For the 6% mortgage payments, it's mostly interest:

$200,000 Mortgage (4.5% APR)
■ Principal: $200,000
  Interest: $164,813

$200,000 Mortgage (6% APR)
■ Principal: $200,000
  Interest: $231,676

54.8%

46.3%

Refinancing only makes sense if you can get a lower interest rate. Another aspect to take into consideration is the various closing fees and other costs associated with refinancing. These typically run into the thousands of dollars, and may not sufficiently offset the savings from lower monthly payments. In addition, be prepared to process a mountain of paperwork — acknowledgements, disclosures, truth-in-lending forms, old tax returns, credit reports, and more.

Is it a mistake to take on debt?

When you take out a mortgage or refinance your home, take on a car loan, utilize store credit or pay for anything using your credit card, you are building up debt. This is money that you have to pay back to a *creditor*, often with interest.

Is taking on debt a mistake? While some hardliners consider all forms of debt to be evil, I am more moderate, and view debt along a spectrum of necessity:

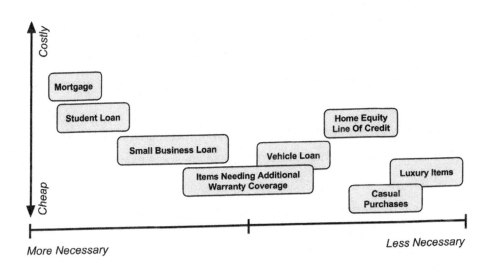

Practically speaking, this means that my family *does* take on debt to pay for things we consider to be necessary, such as a mortgage and student loans. But we have never taken out a car loan, and avoid credit card debt based on casual purchases. We have one credit card that we pay off every month, so interest payments never enter the equation. Recently I have been paying with cash for smaller purchases, as I am less and less convinced that retailers and restaurants are able to keep our information protected from thieves.

A secondary factor that we take into consideration is the benefits associated with having debt.

Wait a minute. *Benefits?*

That's right, benefits. And I am not just talking about the convenience of being able to use plastic to pay for a ribwich down at the local barbecue joint. The debt that we carry comes with the following benefits:

- At tax time, **mortgage interest payments are usually deductible**.

- **Student loan interest payments are usually deductible**.

- Paying off bills and existing debt payments on time can lead to **better credit scores**, which makes it easier to secure loans in the future.

In addition, while not strictly a benefit of having debt, credit cards often offer additional benefits to attract customers. Here are some examples:

- *Insurance associated with purchases*, including refund protection, purchase protection, and extended warranties. If available, the issuer's website or contract will spell out the details of how these work.

- Rental car insurance. This can save hundreds of dollars off of a weekly car rental. Again, check the small print, or call your card issuer to verify whether it's available and how it works.

- Airline miles.

- Points which can be redeemed for cash back rewards or merchandise.

Note that not all credit cards offer these benefits. In addition, some benefits require "premium" card plans that have annual fees or higher interest rates.

While these benefits reduce the pain of taking on debt, they should *never* be seen as a justification for buying a house you can't afford, wasting money on luxuries, spending beyond your means, or building up a mountain of debt that is difficult or impossible to pay back.

Jordan's credit card problem in one easy chart

As mentioned earlier in the guide, Jordan has a spending problem. She can address many of the issues by cutting down on the luxury purchases and performing some emergency surgery on her cable TV plan. But for the debt that she's already incurred on three bank credit cards and several store credit accounts, what's the best approach to take?

Here's how the bank credit cards stack up:

Card	Debt Owed	Rate	Minimum Payment
Megabank MegaBenefits Gold Card	$4,500	19.95%	$300
Explorer TravelMax Card	$5,000	14%	$900
University SmartShopping Rewards	$6,000	22.99%	$1,200

One thing you should understand about Jordan's credit cards: The issuing bank or store *wants* her to pay the minimum. If she pays the minimum, that means the issuer can make more money off the amount that remains, which is subject to the interest rates listed above.

This is where consumer psychology enters the picture. Like many people, Jordan pays off the credit cards with the lowest outstanding balance first. It makes her feel that she's accomplishing something tangible in her fight against debt.

However, she'd actually be much better off tackling the debt with the highest interest rates. Why? Because the higher interest debt grows faster. Indeed, that's exactly what's happened with her University SmartShopping Rewards card, which has the highest rate (nearly 23%) and the highest amount owed ($6,000).

Consolidating credit card debt

One option Jordan has is to consolidate her debt. This basically means using a low-interest credit card to pay off the debt on the high-interest cards. The outstanding balances on the high-interest card are transferred to the lower-interest card, making it easier to pay off the debt.

Here's an actual offer I received in the mail:

Get a promotional rate of 0% APR until May 1, 2015, on balance transfers and convenience checks that post to your account between May 1, 2014, and June 15, 2014. After May 1, 2015, your APR on these balances will be **7.75%.** This APR will vary with the market based on the Prime Rate.

Skip the transaction fees on balance transfers and convenience checks that post to your account by **June 15, 2014.** Each balance transfer and convenience check that posts after this date will receive the regular balance transfer or cash advance fee of just **3% or $75,** whichever is less.

You work hard for your money. Keep more of it in your pocket instead of paying it on interest.

There are some issues with card-based debt consolidation, however:

- There are often transfer fees to contend with, which typically range between 2% and 4%. The above example is 3% after a certain date.

- The rate on some low-interest cards can sometimes balloon to 20% or more after a certain "introductory period", or because of triggers such as late payments.

- Debt consolidation and "credit repair" scams abound. The ads typically appear on the Internet and late-night television. Sometimes scammers even robocall your home! The shady firms promise to deal with creditors on your behalf in return for large fees, but typically do nothing ... or make the problem even worse.

The Federal Trade Commission website (ftc.gov) contains more information on potential scams related to debt consolidation, and also has advice for people with serious debt problems.

How credit ratings agencies "score" you

A credit report is a document that grades you on your ability to pay your bill. The companies that provide the reports — Experian, TransUnion, and Equifax — gather information from the credit card companies, mortgage lenders, department stores, utilities, and other firms that have provided credit to you in the past. The information they gather is aggregated into what's called a FICO score, a number between 350 and 850 that reflects your creditworthiness.

People with lower FICO scores are considered less likely to pay their bills. Mortgage, credit card, telecommunications companies and even some utilities may reject their applications, or may charge higher rates and fees.

Among the population at large, relatively few have terrible credit card scores. The following table shows the distribution of FICO scores among people evaluated by one of the credit rating agencies, TransUnion. More than 50% have a FICO score above 700:

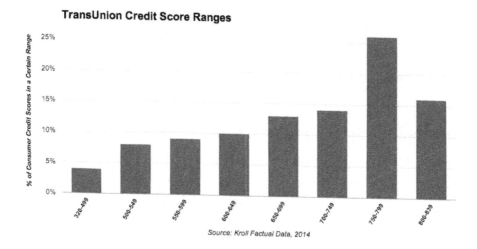

TransUnion Credit Score Ranges

Source: Kroll Factual Data, 2014

How to get a free credit report

Typically, when you apply for a new credit card or mortgage, or want to rent an apartment, the bank, lender, or landlord will run a credit report on you. They want to know if you are likely to pay on time and pay off any debt that you incur.

Wouldn't it be great to see your credit report? It would allow you to understand your credit profile from the view of banks and other issuers, and identify any potential problems that need to be addressed.

Here's some good news: You *can* see your credit report, and it's free, thanks to federal law. Go to the government-operated website usa.gov and look for the links that direct you to an external site that is the only official location to request reports from the three big agencies. Note that the free reports show many details about your credit history, but do *not* show your credit score — that is only available for a fee.

Once you get your report, check it carefully. If you see mistakes such as incorrect information about a dispute, unpaid accounts that you never opened, or other people (and their debt) being associated with you, there are processes for having this information removed.

Be on the lookout for situations that might indicate identity theft. You *will* need to resolve any case of fraud that is wrongly associated with your identity. Further, there are rights you have as a consumer — check out the ftc.gov website to learn more.

What happens when you don't pay your bills

If you can follow some of the advice in this book to reduce spending (both fixed and flexible), it will make paying your remaining bills easier. It may also help you reduce your credit card debt, monthly payments on mortgages, and other obligations.

But what happens if you *still* have trouble making payments? The next few pages cover some of the consequences for failing to pay a bill.

Secured debt vs. unsecured debt

Debt can be classified as *secured* or *unsecured*:

- **Secured debt** is tied to an asset, such as property or a car. For instance, when you take out a mortgage to purchase a house, the house itself becomes collateral for the loan. In other words, it secures the loan. Car loans and some business loans are also structured this way.

- **Unsecured debt** does not have any collateral associated with it. This would include credit cards or merchant credit, as well as student loans and medical bills.

Practically speaking, failing to make payments on secured debt can lead to serious consequences. The bank may take your house away, or repossess your car.

Unsecured creditors use other methods to get some or all of the money that's owed to them. The methods include:

- Adding penalties for failing to pay on time.

- Reporting late payments or failure to pay to credit reporting agencies.

- Starting collection proceedings, including sending notices and making regular phone calls.

- Negotiating a repayment plan.

- Selling the debt to another company, which may make more aggressive attempts to collect.

- Taking you to court, and obtaining a judgment against you.

Depending on the state you live in, judgment creditors may legally force you to reveal information about your income and assets, garnish your wages and bank accounts, and even seize property.

Paying off debt: what to watch out for

If you are in a situation in which secured or unsecured debt has gotten out of control, you need to have a plan for reducing the debt. The process of reducing serious debt is beyond the scope of this guide, but there are a few basic issues to stress:

- Federal law forbids debt collectors from contacting you after certain hours, calling you at work, or continuing to call you after you have sent them a written notice asking them to stop.

- Because the consequences of failing to pay your mortgage are so dire (you can be thrown out of your home!) the Federal Trade Commission *advises contacting your lender immediately*. If your bank thinks the situation is temporary, you may be able to get help suspending or reducing payments, or work out some other sort of plan. Be sure you understand the fees or other financial penalties for doing so.

- If you can't work something out with the lender, contact a *legitimate* housing agency near you. Contact your state housing authority to get a list of agencies.

- If you have serious credit card debt, talk with a *reputable* nonprofit credit counseling agency. Your state attorney general or local consumer protection agency should be able to steer you in the right direction.

- For-profit debt settlement companies may offer to negotiate with creditors on your behalf, but this approach comes with additional risks, complications, and potential scams. Visit the FTC website at *ftc.gov* to learn more.

- Filing for bankruptcy in federal court may get creditors off your back, but it will impact your life for years to come. Depending on the type of bankruptcy, you may have to liquidate all of your assets, leave your home, or come up with a plan to use your future income to pay off your debts. You *must* have credit counseling before filing for bankruptcy and get a certificate from a provider approved by the U.S. Trustee program. Check the U.S. Trustee Program website at *www.usdoj.gov/ust* for more information.

Summary

Fixed expenses are the parts of your household budget that can't be removed. They include obligations such as taxes and health insurance, as well as necessities such as transportation and telecom costs.

While these items can't be eliminated, some are easy to cut, such as expensive cell phone bills. Others can be reduced if conditions allow it, such as refinancing a mortgage or consolidating credit card debt. For other fixed costs, such as car payments, switching from new to used vehicles can make a huge difference.

Finally, letting credit card or other forms of debt get out of control can lead to financial disaster. If debt is starting to become problematic, deal with it as soon as possible. In addition to cutting expenses and paying off or consolidating high-interest credit cards, there are resources that can help you identify problem areas and get advice.

Chapter 4

Managing your accounts & data

The final chapter of this guide deals with how to better organize your bills, financial data, and other records.

Wait a second. There's a whole chapter on *filing* stuff? I can hear you now:

"Bor-ing!"

"Why waste my time on this, if it doesn't affect the bottom line?"

"I already have a system. If it ain't broke, don't fix it!"

Hear me out, people. Filing and organizing *is* a drag. No one likes to deal with paperwork, and some of the technology related to accessing, transferring, and saving computer data can make your head spin.

But organizing your paper and computer records is important and useful. Let me list the reasons why:

- **Some files and data *have* to be retained**. Tax-related filings and documentation are an obvious category. Other types of paperwork should be retained in case of disputes with vendors, so the next time you want to raise hell about mysterious mobile phone charges or file a health insurance claim, you'll be ready.

- **A better system of organizing files and data makes it easy to identify problems and track your progress**. For example, if you have three credit cards, two bank accounts, and regular mortgage and student loan payments, you may not have an accurate picture of your month-to-month spending, savings, and debt levels. Using one of the tools in this chapter can help you track where the money is coming in, where it's going out, and your progress.

- **Once you have systems in place to organize your paper files and computer, they are not hard to maintain.**

Let's take a look at the different methods Frank, Jordan, and Stephanie use to manage their records.

Example A: Frank's paper monster

You may recall that Frank had some pretty major financial issues. He was even evicted from his apartment a few years ago for nonpayment of rent.

Some of Frank's troubles were due to bad spending habits. But another factor has contributed to Frank's troubles: He is terrible at managing his records, which are mostly paper.

How bad is it? Old bills and unopened bank statements are bundled into desk drawers, placed on countertops, or inadvertently thrown out. Receipts are piled on his dresser, or forgotten in his pants pockets. Some paper even ends up in his car, where it is stepped on or stuffed in the glove compartment.

Frank has trouble keeping track of what he owes to various vendors, and frequently misses payments. Sometimes it's because he forgets bills are due, while at other times he can't find the bill and return envelope when he is ready to pay. This leads to added fees and credit card debt, not to mention additional late notices and calls from billing departments. Several times he has had phone service or utilities cut off.

Now that Frank has identified some flexible expenses that can be cut, he will be better able to pay off his bills. But he can make life a lot easier if he gets a better system in place to manage paper records.

Example B: Jordan's online-centric system

Jordan hates clutter. Long ago, she ditched most of her paper bills, bank statements, and payments by check. Now she favors tools and processes that are centered around her online bank account at Megabank.

Her salary, tax refunds, and other incoming payments are deposited electronically into her account. She loves the online bill payment features, and almost never uses her checkbook. On those rare occasions she receives a paper check, she whips out her phone and uses the official Megabank mobile app to take a picture of the check and remotely deposit the funds to her account.

Jordan is living the digital life, and loves it! What more could she possibly want?

While Jordan has been able to cut down her luxury purchases and unnecessary cable TV services, she still hasn't caught up with her debt. She currently has outstanding debt on three credit cards and two department store credit accounts. One of the credit cards is linked to her online bank account, which makes it easier to monitor the debt and payments. But the four other accounts aren't integrated, which makes it hard to keep track of individual payments and overall debt.

Another issue for Jordan is that she doesn't keep good digital records of what's going into her account, and what's being paid out. She can review some payments that have been made through her online bank account, but the records only go back 90 days. And while she pays her taxes electronically, the PDF copies are not always saved or archived. If she ever gets audited, she will have a tough time producing records of important financial transactions. Even if she wants to dispute an electricity bill, she might not be able to track the payment history to the utility.

Example C: Stephanie's smart approach

Stephanie has a different approach to record keeping.

While she uses online banking and direct deposit, she also has gets paper statements and bills from certain vendors, such as her insurance company and 401(k) provider.

Why? She likes the paper reminders, which are hard to ignore compared to email or electronic notifications. She also likes having an actual paper trail of records in case of disputes or questions about particular charges.

For those companies which insist on using online payments, she is careful to generate receipts of transactions. For instance, after paying her mobile phone bill, she prints out the confirmation page. For her online tax filings, she saves a PDF copy of her return and prints out a copy, too.

Stephanie uses some new online tools that help her track her spending habits and savings. Mint.com lets her connect all of her online accounts, including accounts at her bank, her credit card accounts, and her retirement accounts. She can also set up and track monthly budgets by category:

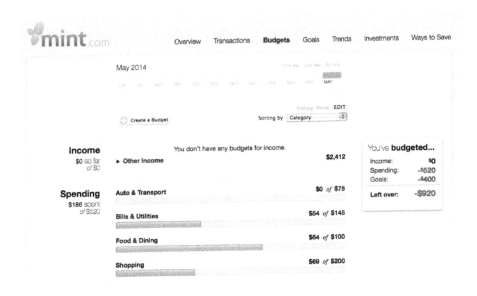

Every time she logs in, Stephanie can see outstanding balances, debt, and other activity that gives her a window into how she's managing her finances. (I'll cover Mint later in this chapter.)

Finally, Stephanie has processes for managing her paper records that make it easy for her to find specific documents months or years after they've been filed away. She also has a system to better manage and back up the digital records on her computer.

Getting smart about paper records

For years, pundits have predicted that it's only a matter of time before everyone shifts to electronic billing and record keeping. Bill Gates, the founder of Microsoft, once dreamed of a "paperless office" where printers, copiers, binders, folders, and other paper records would be retired and replaced by computer disks and online storage systems.

The dream hasn't panned out. While sophisticated personal and business payment systems now exist online, millions of people still prefer to get paper statements in the mail, make payments by check, and operate their businesses using paper records and communications. Some people still use faxes!

My approach takes the best of both worlds: I use online and mobile tools that make it easier to manage my finances, but use paper-based processes which offer additional benefits:

- **Paper lasts longer**. If stored with care, paper records can last decades. Contrast that with digital data, which can be made inaccessible by accidental deletions or account closures, an online company going out of business, or obsolete media (good luck loading that 3.5" floppy disc from 1995!)

- **Simple indexing systems can make retrieval of paper records much easier.**

- **Paper records are easier to review and mark up** if you need to add a reminder or note. Try circling an expense and writing a quick note in the margins of a PDF copy of your credit card statement!

- In the hands of trusted parties, **paper records are less likely to be hacked or stolen** than an email attachment.

- If there is a dispute or question about a charge, paper statements, letters, bills, receipts, and other records **serve as more robust forms of evidence**.

On this last point, I recently had a dispute with my state tax agency about the payment of my corporate income tax. The bureaucrats didn't want a copy of the email from my accountant or the PDF receipt of the transactions — they wanted bank statements and printouts to be *faxed* to them!

Likewise, when I recently refinanced, everything had to be on paper.

Tools to manage paper records

I used to manage my paper records with large manila envelopes. Credit card receipts and statements would be stuffed in the envelope marked "Credit Cards", auto-related paperwork went into the "Car" file, etc.

It was a mess to manage. I ended up with boxes of envelopes that were hard to sort through. The envelopes also started falling apart within a year or two of filling up.

In 2001, I switched to a new system:

- **Important records that I wanted to permanently preserve** (birth certificates, auto titles, passports, insurance policies) were placed in folders and then stored in a fireproof safe. There aren't many of these records, and I only need to open up the safe a few times per year to add or remove items.

- **Paperwork related to my retirement accounts** (monthly statements and transaction records) are kept in jumbo-sized three-ring binders. The binders typically fill up in three years.

Everything else goes into an annual accordion filing box with the following categories:

- **Auto**: Receipts for car repairs, electronic toll statements, etc.

- **Banking**: Monthly checking account and mortgage statements, ATM receipts.

- **Credit Card**: Monthly statements.

- **Financial**: Miscellaneous financial statements and documents.

- **Insurance**: Auto, home, life, and other insurance paperwork.

- **Kids**: Camp, daycare, school records, etc.

- **Medical/Dental**: All bills, pharmacy receipts, and medical records.

- **Miscellaneous**: Anything not easily filed elsewhere.

- **Small receipts**: Small receipts (less than $100) from grocery stores, gas stations, restaurants, and shops.

- **Big receipts**: Purchases of large items that are expensive and/or have warranties.

- **Taxes**: W2 forms and year-end tax statements from any source, records of charitable donations, etc.

- **Travel**: Itineraries, expense receipts, frequent flyer statements, and other records related to domestic and international travel.

- **Utilities**: Phone, gas, water, and other bills related to utilities or recurring home services.

- **Work**: HR paperwork, pay stubs, and other work-related records.

By the end of the year, the accordion file is nearly full. I get a new one for the new year (they cost less than $15 at the local office supply store), and store the old accordion file on a high shelf in the basement.

The beauty of the system is that it's clear where everything has to go, and it's easy to find specific records based on the category and the year it was filed. More than once I have dug into an old accordion file to dig up old tax records. Recently I had to look in the files for 2009 to find the receipt for an appliance that had broken down. I used the receipt to receive free warranty repairs.

Destroying old records

While I could keep the accordion files forever, it's not necessary for most types of paper records. Experts advise keeping tax records for 6 years, the length of time the IRS has to audit you if you underreport your income by 25% or more.

I actually keep tax and other important records for much longer. To determine when to destroy old bills, bank statements, and other paper records, I apply a common-sense protocol:

- The contents of accordion files are kept for 6 years.
- After 6 years, all tax records are removed from the accordion file and put into long-term storage boxes.
- Financial records from retirement accounts are also kept in long-term storage.
- All records of medical diagnoses or reports (including kids' vaccinations) are placed in my fireproof safe.
- Bank and credit card records, social security earnings reports, and records containing private or otherwise valuable information are shredded, using a $20 plug-in shredder that fits on top of a wastebasket.
- Everything else goes in the paper recycling bin.

Most of the paper records from the accordion files are eventually shredded or recycled. Only the important stuff — tax records, medical histories, and some financial records — are kept longer.

The accordion files can be reused if they are still in good condition.

Tools to manage personal data & computer files

Most people don't have a system for organizing their computer files. Attachments, documents, PDFs and electronic receipts tend to be stored willy-nilly on PC desktops or removable storage, such as USB drives. You may even have old CDs or floppy disks lying around with data on them.

The situation is compounded by the fact that PCs and laptops are typically replaced every 3 or 4 years. If the old computer is not broken, it may be sold, donated, or stuffed into the back of a closet. The data on them is not always transferred, saved, or destroyed.

In this section, I have some basic advice for organizing, saving, and preserving data. Note that *securing* data is also important, but it goes beyond the scope of this guide (except for a short section on password selection — see "Jordan's dumb password").

The system I use on my personal computer is similar to my paper system, in that much of the data is organized by year and then by topic and subtopic. For instance, I have a directory on my computer titled "2014 Home" with subfolders for the following:

- Banking
- Correspondence
- Education
- Misc.
- Taxes

Similarly, there is a folder titled "2014 Work" which contains any work-related receipts or records that have been sent by email or need to be stored electronically.

For digital photos and videos, I use the default software that comes with the computer to view the files. However, I have a system of folders based on the year the photos were taken (for instance, "2014 Summer" or "2014 Mom's

Birthday"). Many photo programs also allow photos to be tagged by name, event, or another attribute. A few programs automatically organize photos based on simple facial recognition and the photo's metadata (digitally generated geographical information that describes where and when a photo was taken).

Data is constantly being backed up. This means creating a copy of files, photos, and important programs. If my computer dies, I can use the most recent backup to restore my files once the computer is fixed or replaced.

How to back up your computer data

Books have been written about how to effectively back up your data. In fact, I wrote one of them — *Dropbox In 30 Minutes*!

Dropbox is an Internet-based system for backing up your data and photographs. While Dropbox is very convenient (most of the backups automatically take place in the background), there are some security considerations which make me wary of using it for sensitive data. For instance, I do not store banking information or old tax returns on Dropbox.

Many people use external hard disk drives to back up and store the data on their PCs. The drives are the size of a thick paperback book, and can be tucked behind the PC or off to the side. Here's how they work:

- The drives are cheap (less than $100 for smaller units). They are so cheap, that you can have more than one. I have two units — one that's attached to my laptop for daily backups (see image, below), and another drive that I back up to every year and then store in the fireproof safe I mentioned earlier.

- The drives typically connect to the PCs via a USB cable for fast file transfers.

- They can store terabytes of data, which is the equivalent of hundreds of thousands of digital files, photos, and programs.

- If your drives don't already have their own storage management software installed, your computer probably has a simple utility to help manage regular backups and set security and encryption settings.

If you don't have a large amount of data to back up, there are simpler solutions available, such as encrypted USB drives. Other people use

Dropbox or similar services such as Microsoft OneDrive.

People who have serious storage or security requirements may use advanced home networking systems and hardware appliances to back up their data. As this subtopic is complicated and goes well beyond the scope of this guide, your best bet is to go on the Web and search for "home networking systems" to learn more.

Digital tools for managing & tracking your finances

The following section describes some online tools and processes that can help you better manage your finances. This is by no means a complete list, but is intended to give you an idea of what's available.

In addition, while there are many helpful data protection tools available, it's ultimately up to you to be smart about security. This means not only using strong passwords and having backup email addresses and phone numbers, but also being aware of scams, tricks, and two-faced friends accessing your data without your permission.

Let's start with a short discussion about choosing passwords to protect your online data and identity.

Jordan's dumb password

Jordan has a problem. She has made a grave mistake in the password that she uses for her email, social media accounts, online banking, Amazon, and every other online and mobile service that she has signed up for. Here's the password:

JM071987

Jordan thinks this is a great password. It's easy to remember, has a mix of letters and numbers, and looks kind of "random" to anyone who happens to see it. She thinks it's a lot smarter than some of the other passwords that people use, like "password123" or the names of pets and children.

It's actually a pretty dumb password. The letters and numbers aren't random at all — they are Jordan's initials and the month and year of her birth. Someone who knows her could guess it, and smart hackers who know her name (easily found on Facebook) could apply various techniques to figure out her password.

There's another big problem with Jordan's password. Not only is it easy to guess, she uses it on every website and mobile app she has registered for. This means if someone guesses or steals her password for one service, they have the keys to the castle for every other service she uses, including critical services such as email and bank accounts.

What should Jordan do? As a first step, she should immediately change all of her important passwords. Here are some criteria that she could apply when choosing new passwords:

- Each account that contains personal or important data should have a unique password. The same goes for four-digit personal identification numbers (PINs).
- Don't use first or last names, initials, or common words — *especially* "password".
- Don't use repeated or consecutive numbers ("123456" or "8888").
- Include a mix of letters (upper and lower case) as well as numbers

and (if allowed) symbols.

- If asked to create answers to security questions, avoid questions which have answers that can be easily found out, such as place of birth, elementary school, or mother's maiden name.

- Leave a backup email address or a mobile phone number, which can help with password recovery.

- Change passwords regularly.

- Store passwords in a secure place (*not* on a piece of paper in a desk drawer!)

Anyone who is serious about account security should also use "two-factor identification" when it is offered. If enabled, when someone tries to log on to the account from an unrecognized device or location, that person will not only have to enter the password, they will also have to enter a code that's sent to the mobile phone associated with the account. It is a bit of an inconvenience, but it makes it extremely difficult for hackers or scheming ex-boyfriends or girlfriends to access email or social media accounts.

Hidden features of online banking

Almost everyone knows about online banking. It's a Web-based system for accessing a list of recent transactions and other basic information about an account. There are also common features such as online bill payments, which let people send checks or electronic payments to vendors.

Not all online banking systems are created equal, however. Your small local bank may cover the basics, but the big national banks often have more sophisticated features. In addition, certain banks may require account minimums or charge a monthly fee to access services such as Bill Pay.

Here is a list of online features that are typically offered by banks:

- **Mobile deposits**: Use an app on your mobile phone to take pictures of checks, and remotely deposit them. This eliminates having to go to the bank in person to make the deposit.

- **Mobile alerts**: Set up alerts that will be sent as a text message to your phone. The alerts can be regular balance updates, or a confirmation of a transaction such as a big deposit or withdrawal.

- **Automated online transfers**: Set up regular transfers between two of your accounts. A typical example is a monthly transfer from your checking account to your mortgage account. This eliminates having to mail in the check, and also avoids late fees. But make sure the checking account has enough money, or you may get socked with an overdraft fee.

- **Automated checks**: Send a check every month to a certain party, such as a service provider or relative.

- **Online travel settings**: If a bank or credit card issuer notices that a customer's card has been used in another state or country, it may flag the transaction as suspicious or suspend the card ... unless the customer has given notice in advance of planned travel. Online travel settings let you notify your bank online, without having to call up during business hours.

- **Reward points**: If you have a bank-issued credit card that is tied to some sort of rewards program, you can use various online features to manage the points. Typically, people may "cash in" their points once they reach a certain level, or exchange them for merchandise.

Finally, a few larger banks offer money management features to help you better budget and plan your spending. You can usually see how much you are spending in each category (see image, below). There are often more advanced tools, including the ability to set targets in certain categories (for instance, $200 per month in restaurant expenditures) as well as alerts when your spending gets close to or goes over the target.

However, the money management features are sometimes held back by the fact that they only cover the accounts at the bank that offers the features. If you have more than one bank, or want to see how spending takes place across multiple bank, credit card, and financial services accounts, you may be interested in the personal money management tools offered by Quicken, Mint, and others. I'll cover the basics in the next section.

Should I use Quicken, Mint, or something else?

Quicken, Mint, Check, and other services offer the ability to aggregate and track all of your financial and spending information in one place.

The basic idea behind these services is similar. After registering, provide the login details for various accounts — banking, credit card, loans, bills, etc. The software connects to these accounts, downloads the data, and adds everything up. The software interfaces can display the following data:

- Total cash available, across all accounts

- Total credit available

- Monthly budgets and expenditures, by category

- Investment performance (stocks, mutual funds, retirement accounts, etc.)

- Alerts (for instance, a spike in spending in a certain category, or an upcoming bill)

- Advanced features such as investment analysis and online payments

If you complete the setup process and link up all of your primary bank, credit card, and financial services accounts, these tools can provide some fascinating insights into your assets, investments, and spending levels. One of the most eye-opening pieces of information for me was a chart on Mint.com that showed my overall assets, including the total value of my house and retirement accounts.

But the services have some fundamental differences:

Application	Main Platform	Cost	Notes
Quicken	Desktop PC	Basic: $40	Robust features. Data stored on PC.
Mint	Online	Free	Great online interface. Solid budgeting features.
Check	Mobile	Free	Allows bill payments via slick mobile app.

(Note: Mint.com is now owned by Intuit, which also sells Quicken as well as other financial software packages including TurboTax and Quickbooks.)

Many people would choose one of the free money management tools. However, there are a lot of people who will gladly pay for Quicken *because* it is PC-based software. Data you enter into Quicken is not uploaded to the Internet. This means users have more control over their data, and feel reassured that all of their sensitive personal and financial information won't reside on a remote server or in the cloud.

In addition, users of Mint and Check have reported issues with third-party bank and billing accounts that may become inaccessible or fail to update. Being unable to access certain data makes for flawed planning and analysis. For instance, how can you accurately track and plan for debt reduction if you can't connect to all of your credit card accounts?

Lastly, the services can be complicated. Besides the hassles associated with connecting all of your accounts, setting up budgets, targets, and alerts is a lengthy process. Some people have complained that the tools aren't flexible enough to handle real-world budgeting or planning situations that might be thrown off by an emergency or unexpected expense.

PayPal, Dwolla, and alternative payment systems

If you use eBay or have paid someone over the Internet, you're probably familiar with PayPal. The basic PayPal service lets people pay another PayPal account holder almost instantly. It's an alternative to paying someone by check, or via cash.

The setup for PayPal and alternative services such as Dwolla is straightforward:

- Enter your bank account information

- Wait a few days for the accounts to be connected

- Confirm that several small electronic funds transfers have taken place — typically a few pennies are deposited into your bank account, which verifies to PayPal, Dwolla, or competing services that the account is yours.

- Transfer some of your bank funds to the PayPal or Dwolla account. You will be able to use these funds to pay other people who have an account with the same service.

The services have different fee structures:

- PayPal transfers between private parties are supposed to be free, but business-related transactions are charged a fee that totals about 3% of the transaction.

- Dwolla doesn't charge anything for basic transfers, but has fee-based services for priority support and other features.

The services are convenient, and I have used both PayPal and Dwolla for my business. However, there are definite drawbacks:

- Each service requires both the sending and receiving parties to have active accounts with the same service, and connected bank accounts. This means if you want to pay someone right away, and they *don't* have an account, it will take that person at least three or four days to get the account set up and connected with his or her bank. In that time, you could easily write and send a check.

- Although the services are *supposed* to be easy to set up, many people have trouble getting their bank accounts connected or performing other basic functions.

- Because online payment systems have been abused by fraudsters and organized crime, these companies are often overzealous about sudden, unexplained flows of money. PayPal is notorious for freezing legitimate accounts and making it nearly impossible to quickly access frozen funds.

Many people have understandable qualms about trusting their bank information to a Web-based service that will store the data remotely. Conceivably, a lot of money can be instantly lost if passwords and other credentials are stolen.

Conclusion

Over the past 30 minutes, we've learned about some basic personal finance concepts. I sincerely hope the advice in this guide can help you better manage spending and ultimately help you spend more time (and money) on the things that matter most to you and your family.

What's next? There is a follow-up guide titled *Personal Finance For Beginners In 30 Minutes, Vol. 2: How to build savings and investments to support current needs and retirement planning*. The purpose of the second volume is to show how your savings can be leveraged for near-term needs as well as long-term financial goals. The guide includes sections about:

- Buying a home

- Establishing a special savings accounts for emergencies

- Why Social Security isn't enough for retirement

- The pros and cons of 401(k) plans, IRA accounts, and other types of retirement savings vehicles

- Mutual fund basics, from compounding to index funds

Personal Finance For Beginners In 30 Minutes, Vol. 2 also includes examples featuring our favorite workplace trio, Frank, Jordan, and Stephanie. We'll see how they learn how to fund special savings accounts, leverage matching retirement contributions from their employers, and perform other savings-related tasks that can help secure their financial futures.

To order *Personal Finance For Beginners In 30 Minutes, Vol. 2*, please visit personalfinance.in30minutes.com. The website also includes blog posts, tips, and other personal finance resources.

A request for readers

Thanks for reading *Personal Finance For Beginners In 30 Minutes, Vol. 1!* This guide was created to help people better manage their money, and I hope it has given you some practical ideas that you can apply to your own finances.

I would like to ask you to take a few minutes right now to rate and review the guide. Reviews can be left on the following sites:

- Amazon product page

- Google Play product page

- B&N product page

- Apple iBookstore product page

- Goodreads.com

If you are interested in learning more about personal finance topics, or ordering Vol. 2 (which covers savings and retirement planning), please visit the official companion website to this guide, located at personalfinance.in30minutes.com. You can also download the PDF version of *Personal Finance For Beginners In 30 Minutes, Vol. 2* for free as part of the In 30 Minutes Starter Library by signing up for our monthly newsletter. Go to in30minutes.com/newsletter for more details.

Thanks again!

Ian Lamont (ian@in30minutes.com)

Bonus: Introduction to iPhone 6 & iPhone 6S In 30 Minutes

The following chapter is excerpted from iPhone 6 & iPhone 6S In 30 Minutes. If you're interested in downloading the ebook or purchasing the paperback, please visit the guide's official website, googledrive.in30minutes.com.

For many people, getting a new iPhone is almost like buying a car. It's not just because the devices are expensive and constantly used. Buyers get wrapped up in the whole experience. They obsessively compare specs, spend hours reading reviews, and even check out people unboxing the phones on YouTube. Then, it's time to turn on the phone and customize it ... and show off the shiny new toy to friends, coworkers, family members, and any other captive audience!

That's certainly been the experience for me. And even if you don't get excited about a new phone release, the devices that make up Apple's iPhone 6 family are nevertheless impressive pieces of engineering and design. Consider the following features:

	iPhone 6	iPhone 6 Plus	iPhone 6S	iPhone 6S Plus
Weight	4.6 oz/129 grams	6.1 oz/172 grams	5 oz/143 grams	6.8 oz/192 grams
Display (diagonal)	4.7 inches	5.5 inches	4.7 inches	5.5 inches
Resolution	1334 x 750 pixels	1920 x 1080 pixels	1334 x 750 pixels	1920 x 1080 pixels
Processor	A8	A8	A9	A9
iSight camera	8 Megapixel	8 Megapixel	12 Megapixel	12 Megapixel
FaceTime camera	1.2 Megapixel	1.2 Megapixel	5 Megapixel	5 Megapixel
Video recording	1080p HD	1080p HD	4K	4K
Max. talk time (3G)	14 hours	24 hours	14 hours	24 hours

Apple's mobile operating system — iOS — is also well-designed, and comes with new features that extend the usefulness of the device. Imagine paying for something simply by holding up a phone to a credit card terminal, and pressing your finger against a fingerprint reader. It sounds like something out of a futuristic novel or TV show, yet it's possible now for owners of any iPhone 6 model.

There are many ways to use the new phones. Here are some sample profiles of iPhone 6 users:

Renata is a mom by day and a restaurant hostess by night. She uses text messaging, Facebook, and Apple's video conferencing technology called FaceTime to keep in touch with her friends and coordinate activities for her sons. While driving to work, she plays podcasts on her iPhone 6, which is connected to her car's stereo speakers. Once she gets to the restaurant, she goes to her iPhone's calendar app to arrange her work schedule, using a shared work calendar.

Harlan is a junior at the local community college, majoring in biology. He depends on his large-screen iPhone 6 Plus to keep in touch with classmates, using social media applications such as Snapchat and Instagram. Harlan also uses the Google Docs app to prepare homework assignments and collaborate on reports, and he can actually type using a portable Bluetooth keyboard that he pairs with his phone. Entertainment options include Apple Music and a slew of games, including his favorite time-waster, Plants vs. Zombies.

Corlis works in the finance department of a large retail chain. Her work-issued iPhone 6S comes with the mobile versions of Microsoft Word, Microsoft Excel, and a financial calculator, all downloaded from the Apple App Store. Other apps on her phone include Slack, a group communications app, Wunderlist, a sophisticated to-do list, and Dropbox, a cloud storage app which allows her to access and share files saved to her desktop computer. When she's on the road and needs to relax, she switches on an app that plays gentle background sounds such as falling rain and distant wind chimes.

Les is a retired postal clerk and grandfather. He likes to share photos with his family using the sharing features of the Photos app. He is especially fond of the snapshots taken by his 10-year-old granddaughter. For entertainment, he turns to the official NBA app to keep track of his favorite team, and also plays word jumble games against friends living in other states. When he's having his afternoon coffee at the kitchen table, he will use his iPhone to watch streaming video through the Netflix app.

Tom owns a printing business in his hometown. The most crucial iPhone 6S feature for him is Siri, Apple's built-in "personal assistant" which allows him to use the phone without even looking at the screen. Siri can understand spoken commands to get directions to customers' addresses, dial suppliers on his contact list, and even compose text messages.

While the latest phones are powerful and loaded with all kinds of capabilities, there is a learning curve. This is especially true for new iPhone owners who have never used a smartphone, or those who are used to models featuring Android or Windows mobile operating systems. Even if you are migrating from an older iPhone, be aware that the iPhone 6 handles certain tasks differently. The new iPhone models also offer a boatload of new (and obscure) features that need to be explored. While this guide does not cover every feature, it is intended to smooth the learning curve and help you get the most out of your iPhone 6/6 Plus/6S/6S Plus.

We only have 30 minutes, so let's get started!

To learn more about this guide, or to purchase the ebook or paperback edition, please visit iphone.in30minutes.com.

Bonus: Introduction to LinkedIn In 30 Minutes

The following bonus chapter is the introduction to LinkedIn In 30 Minutes (2nd Edition), by author Angela Rose. To download the ebook or purchase the paperback, visit the book's official website, linkedin.in30minutes.com.

I'm going to let you in on a little secret: I haven't always been on LinkedIn. In fact, I wasn't even aware the professional networking platform existed until 2006.

At the time, I was working as a manager in the creative department of a small marketing company. Our clients were primarily in the mortgage and real estate industries, and they would personalize the postcards and newsletters my team and I had created with their logos and contact information before mailing them to their databases. One day a real estate agent asked us to include the web address (or URL) for his LinkedIn profile.

I was intrigued. While I was not a social media newbie — I posted hilarious, adorable and poignant pictures of my cats on Facebook almost every day — the concept of social network for professional people was different. I checked out the agent's profile, took a quick tour of LinkedIn's features, and left it at that. I had a job I loved. I was going to work there until I died. I didn't need what LinkedIn had to offer.

Then the housing bubble burst, causing property values to plummet and thousands of homeowners to default on their mortgages. No one could buy, no one could sell — and our client base began to contract. As we put raises on hold and closed our offices on Fridays, I had to face an unpleasant reality: It was very possible I'd need to find a new job — or strike out on my own — in the near future.

Suddenly, being on LinkedIn looked like a really good idea. I spent 30 minutes that first Friday setting up a free profile. While I only filled out the basics, I felt better having done something that might help me if the unthinkable happened. About one year later, it did. But by then I had built the foundations of a freelance writing and editing business. I had more than a dozen regular clients, and their assignments were enough, along with some savings, to ensure I'd be able to keep paying my bills (and feeding those cats) as I continued to grow The Quirky Creative.

LinkedIn helped me make it happen. I made a habit of connecting with the decision-makers at every company that used my services. This kept me front of mind, and resulted in referrals and repeat assignments. I asked for — and gave — recommendations, then shared the glowing endorsements with potential clients. This helped me to land more assignments. I added a professional photo, packed my background summary with keywords and personality, and uploaded clips from my growing portfolio of published work.

With every enhancement, my profile received more views. I received more emails from professionals and companies interested in the services I provided. I landed more assignments — and I was able to maintain the lifestyle to which my cats were accustomed (i.e. gourmet kibble, frequent catnip binges and all the toy mice they could shove under the sofa).

In fact, LinkedIn actually led to the book you are reading today. The publisher of In 30 Minutes guides found my profile, liked the contents, and offered me the opportunity to share what I've learned about using this increasingly important social media platform with all of you — no cat photos required!

Not just an online resume

As the above anecdote illustrates, LinkedIn is more than just an online catalog of former employers and responsibilities. It's a tool that can have a significant — and positive — impact on your life, whether you use it to search for a new job, network with other professionals in your industry, establish an online presence or even learn more about potential vendors and service providers (I used it to 'vet' my cats' veterinarian).

Consider the following numbers:

- LinkedIn has approximately 400 million members, located in practically every country in the world. Whether you want to connect with a former supervisor, a colleague you met at a conference, the recruiter at your dream company, or even your old high school track coach (go Warriors!), you are likely to find them on LinkedIn.

- According to a recent LinkedIn report, the network hosts more than 3 million active job listings. Advertised positions are in dozens of industries ranging from agriculture and construction to finance and healthcare. Whatever your area of expertise, you are likely to find employment opportunities on LinkedIn.

- A 2014 Jobvite Social Recruiting Survey found that 93% of recruiters use or plan to use social media platforms to fill jobs. Among these recruiters, 94% use LinkedIn. Whether you are actively searching for a new job or are a passive candidate — defined as interested in opportunities though not active in the job search — joining LinkedIn will make it easier for employers to find you.

How are people leveraging LinkedIn?

While students and recent college grads are the fastest growing demographic on LinkedIn, the social media network has more than 80 million members between the ages of 30 and 49, and more than 100 million who are 50 years of age or older.

How are they using their profiles? Here are just a few examples:

- **Matthew is an account rep for a large biopharma company**. A frequent trade show attendee, he uses LinkedIn to learn more about the professionals he plans to network with on his trips ... and later uses LinkedIn to maintain connections afterward. This has helped him land new accounts as well as forge relationships that may prove valuable when it's time to take the next step in his career.

- **Samantha is a recent college graduate with a degree in human resources management**. She is currently interviewing for jobs as a payroll administrator, and she uses LinkedIn to learn more about the companies she is visiting as well as the professionals conducting the interviews. Thanks to the keywords in her profile, she has been approached by a number of recruiters for jobs she otherwise wouldn't have heard about.

- **John is a freelance graphic designer**. While he hasn't had a regular 9-to-5 job in the last decade, he has used the experience section of his LinkedIn profile to feature several of his current and former contract projects. With dozens of recommendations and hundreds of endorsements, his profile enhances his professional reputation.

- **Amanda was laid off in December**. She has been using LinkedIn to search for a new job in the healthcare industry. A registered nurse, she has connected with the hiring managers at several local hospitals using InMail. She is a member of a half-dozen nursing- and healthcare-related groups and regularly participates in discussions to increase her visibility. She has also spent time enhancing her LinkedIn profile with a current, professional photo and keywords to improve her search ranking.

• **Robert is a retired fireman**. He's not interested in going back to work full-time, or even part-time for that matter, but he likes to see what former colleagues are doing and stay current on the latest industry news. He uses LinkedIn to connect with other public safety professionals, learn new information about the field, and share his experience and opinions with the members of related discussion groups.

Are you ready to get started?

Whatever your age, profession, or employment status, you are almost certain to benefit from learning to use LinkedIn — and doing so is surprisingly easy. It doesn't matter if you are a complete newbie or a frequent social media consumer, this guide will show you how to navigate the LinkedIn platform, register for a free account, set up your profile step-by-step, connect with other members, join discussion groups and search for jobs — all in the time it would take to watch a dozen YouTube cat videos. We only have 30 minutes, so let's get started!

If you're interested in learning more about this title, or buying the ebook or paperback, visit the official website located at linkedin.in30minutes.com.

Bonus: Introduction to Google Drive & Docs In 30 Minutes

The following bonus chapter is the introduction to Google Drive & Docs In 30 Minutes, *by author Ian Lamont. If you're interested in downloading the ebook or purchasing the paperback, please visit the guide's official website,* googledrive.in30minutes.com.

Thanks for your interest in *Google Drive & Docs In 30 Minutes*. I wrote this unofficial user guide to help people get up to speed with Google Drive, a remarkable (and free) online office suite that includes a word processor (Docs), spreadsheet program (Sheets), and slideshow tool (Slides). The guide also covers the storage features of Google Drive.

How do people use Google Drive and Docs? There are many possible uses. Consider these examples:

- **A harried product manager needs to continue work on an important proposal over the weekend**. In the past, she would have dug around in her purse to look for an old USB drive she uses for transferring files. Or, she might have emailed herself an attachment to open at home. Instead, she saves the Word document and an Excel spreadsheet to Google Drive at the office. Later that evening, on her home PC, she opens her Google Drive folder to access the Excel file. All of her saves are updated to Google Drive. When she returns to work the following Monday, the updated data can be viewed on her workstation.

- **The organizer of a family reunion wants to survey 34 cousins** about attendance, lodging preferences, and potluck dinner preparation (always a challenge — the Nebraska branch of the family won't eat corn or Garbanzo beans). He emails everyone a link to a Web Form created in Google Drive. The answers are automatically transferred to Google Sheets, where he can see the responses and tally the results.

- **A small business consultant is helping the owner of Slappy's Canadian Diner** ("We Put The Canadian Back In Bacon") prepare a slideshow for potential franchisees in Ohio. The consultant and Slappy collaborate using Google Slides, which lets them remotely access the deck and add text, images, and other elements. The consultant shares a link to the slideshow with her consulting partner, so he can periodically review it on a Web browser and check for problems. Later, Slappy meets his potential franchise operators at a hotel in Cleveland, and uses Slides to give them his pitch.

- **An elementary school faculty uses Google Docs to collaborate on lesson plans**. Each teacher accesses the same document from their homes or classrooms. Updates are instantly reflected, even when two teachers are simultaneously accessing the same document. Their principal (known as "Skinner" behind his back) is impressed by how quickly the faculty completes the plans, and how well the curriculums are integrated.

- At the same school, **the 5th-grade teachers ask their students to submit homework using Docs**. The teachers add corrections and notes, which the students can access at any time via a Web browser. It's much more efficient than emailing attachments around, and the students don't need to bug their parents to buy expensive word-processing programs.

Many people try Google Docs because it's free (Google Drive is, too, if you store less than five gigabytes of data). Microsoft Office can cost hundreds of dollars. While Google Docs is not as sophisticated, it handles the basics very well. Docs also offers a slew of powerful online features that are unmatched by Office or Apple's iWork suite, including:

- The ability to review the history of a specific document, and revert to an earlier version.

- Simple Web forms and online surveys that can be produced without programming skills or website hosting arrangements.

- Collaboration features that let users work on the same document in real time.

- Offline file storage that can be synced to multiple computers.

- Automatic notification of the release date of Brad Pitt's next movie.

I'm just kidding about the last item. But Google Drive and Docs really can do those other things, and without the help of your company's IT department or the pimply teenager from down the street. These features are built right into the software, and are ready to use as soon as you've signed up.

Even though the myriad features of Google Drive may seem overwhelming, this guide makes it easy to get started. Google *Drive & Docs In 30 Minutes* is written in plain English, with lots of step-by-step instructions, screenshots and tips. Videos and other resources are available on the companion website to this book, googledrive.in30minutes.com. You'll get up to speed in no time.

We've only got a half-hour, so let's get started with Google Drive and Docs!

If you're interested in learning more about this title, or buying the ebook or paperback, visit the official website located at googledrive.in30minutes.com.

CPSIA information can be obtained at www.ICGtesting.com
Printed in the USA
BVOW06s1339090716

454997BV00021B/170/P